by Laura Chester:

Tiny Talk (1972)
The All Night Salt Lick (1972)
Nightlatch (1974)
Primagravida (1975)
Chunk Off & Float (1978)
Watermark (1978)
Proud & Ashamed (1978)
My Pleasure (1980)
Lupus Novice (1987)
Free Rein (1988)

Editor:

Rising Tides, 20th Century American Women Poets (1973)
Deep Down, The New Sensual Writing by Women (1988)

LAURA CHESTER

IN THE

ZONE

NEW
AND
SELECTED
WRITING

BLACK SPARROW PRESS ■ SANTA ROSA ■ 1988

ACKNOWLEDGMENTS

The poems and stories in this book are drawn from the following collections: *Nightlatch*, The Tribal Press, 1974; *Primagravida*, Christopher's Books, 1975; *Chunk Off & Float*, Cold Mountain Press, 1978; *Proud & Ashamed*, Christopher's Books, 1978; *My Pleasure*, The Figures, 1980; *Lupus Novice*, Station Hill Press, 1987 and *Free Rein*, Burning Deck, 1988. Earlier versions of some of these poems have appeared in *Best Friends; Measure; Quetzal; Southern Poetry Review; Stooge; Truck; Nevermind; Poetry Now; ZZZZ; How(Ever); Periodics; Gnome Baker; Notus; Multiples; Velvet Glove; Gravida; Networks; Cream City; Redstart; Rising Tides: 20th Century American Women Poets; I Hear My Sisters Saying; Women: Portraits; 50 Contemporary Poets; 19 New American Poets of the Golden Gate; Up Late: American Poetry Since 1970; Everyday Life; Deep Down: The New Sensual Writing by Women.*

This project is funded in part by the California Arts Council, a state agency. Any findings, opinions, or conclusions contained therein are not necessarily those of the California Arts Council.

LIBRARY OF CONGRESS CATALOGING-IN-PUBLICATION DATA

Chester, Laura.
  In the zone.

  I. Title.
PS3553.H43I5   1988   811'.54   88-7530
ISBN 0-87685-748-9
ISBN 0-87685-749-7 (autographed)
ISBN 0-87685-747-0 (pbk.)

for Margaret Sheftall Chester

"What does it feel like to be *on* playing tennis? Well, you don't feel anything, because you don't know it. You just keep hitting great shots one after another. It's called *being in the zone,* and you just don't miss."

— William Sherman

Table of Contents

NIGHTLATCH (1972-1974)

Faster   15
Art   16
Both Masks Claim Mine   17
Place de l'Ancienne Boucherie   18
Deposit   19
The Recipe   20
Mating Melody   21
Suckle Sex   22
Going Out   23
Suspicion   24
Saint Sanity   25
Post Date   26
Hotel Comfort   27
Those Who Belong Together   28
Shut Down Shut Down Twice   30
What You Eat   31

MUSICAL NEWS (1970-1978)

Wish for Water   35
Deserted   38
July   40
Retired Farmer's Prayer   41
Eyes of the Garden   42
The Woman Who's Trapped Beneath the Seasons   44
The Woman with Love Child   45
The Unmarried Woman Giving Her Child Up for Adoption   46
The Woman Who Went Along With It   47
The Woman Who Chose Abortion   48
The Woman Whose Child Is Born Dead   49
The Woman With Too Many Children Already   50
The Woman Who Takes Care of Other People's Children   51
Dear Helen   52
Dear Geoff   53
Dear Lyle   54
Dear Laura   55

Dear Stan   56
Dear Jill   57
Dear Kate   58
Pavanne for the Passing of a Child   59
Coming Clean   62
Last Breath   65
Goodnight Moon   66
Formal Feeling   67
Memory   68
Simply   69
The Fear   70
Lost Dog   73
Until Death, Do It   76

TRELLIS (1978–1985)

On the Wallowy   85
The Dog the Cat the Bird & the Kid   92
Memory, the Meat Flower   102
Gate's Waiting   104
Trellis   108
In a Motion   112
Iscador   113
Returning to the World   114
Go Round   116

INNER EVEREST (1985–1986)

From: Free Rein   119
In Regard to Him   124
The Feast   127
Partners   128
Eating Alone   130
On the Scent   132
Winter/Shifting   134
Ashcroft   136
Cupid's Hunting Fields   137
The Fawn   139
Relapse   140
Up Until Now   141
What He Likes   142
Sequence   143

Even Too Much Is Not Enough 145
Holy Mackerel 146
Final Proof 148
The Good Time Is Now 150
Speak to Him 151
Swan Song 152
Inner Everest 154

LOVE NOTES TO AN IMPOSSIBLE PERSON (1986–1987)

Love Notes to an Impossible Person 159
Frame 161
Here in Heaven 162
Return Flight 163
Crazy 164
Frozen Heart 166
Strange Streams 167
If They Can Put One Man on the Moon, Why Not
    All of Them 169
Incidental 170
Never Trust a Bachelor Over Forty in the Fast Lane 171
I Hate Your Guts 172
Dreadful 173
Looking for the Exit 174

BEYOND DIVORCED (1987–1988)

Car Pool 179
Time & The Right Time 181
Broken Home 182
Far Be It 183
Weekend People 184
The Lily 186
On the Mend 188
Why I Never Travel Light 190
Whose Arms 191
Loving My Boys 193
Revenge 194
Beyond Divorced 196
Serial 199
Correspondence 200
Love Chant 201

In the Zone   202
Back Together   207

CONVERSATIONS AT BAY (1988)

His Sweater   211
The Introduction   213
The Answer   216
The Trap   218
How to Get Your Own Way   224
Who Knows   227

Letter to Rain   229

Nightlatch
(1972–1974)

Faster

Up there on the mudflats is the most beautiful horse— Free and wild, never been ridden. I catch him in the hallway. He has nowhere to go— Can't escape me now. He quivers all over with sleekness and excitement. I smooth the glistening skin and he stretches his neck, responds to my hand with a whinny after each caress. He will take me to amazing places, and I can trust him without even saddle or bridle. He knows how to climb the air. He is faster than all of the others. So am I. He says, That's how we came to find each other.

Art

I'm very courageous— Going into the deep freezer to store
vegetables in white paper cartons, last used for the goldfish. I work
fast, snapping corn cobs in half, coming out like the snowball you
saved for summer. I lob it at the cook. Why does she have to be
so serious, arranging big leaves of romaine lettuce in tall crystal
glasses. I say, No one's going to eat that! My food's just there for
decoration, she snaps, and besides you aren't invited. Why not?
Just look at yourself. Take a look at those pants— They won't stay
up. Well why don't you model the dessert after me? I get into a
contorted position. She rushes to her drawing board and makes
a cherry pie.

Both Masks Claim Mine

They would call this— Putting on one's face then waiting for a party. But perhaps my friend and I are merely getting ready for each other. The *maquillage* slides onto my cheeks, top cream with a golden glow, rubbing my face to a shimmer to an opal. Skin loses its flesh-like nature, without a pore, clouded out, curled over, becoming the lapped *crème fraîche* of my Normandy. And the bright red kiss of wet enamel is saved on my lips— For whom? My friend and I float about the room, so formal, as if guarding our appearances for the moment of the doorbell. She is seriously considering her breasts, trying to see how they should be laid into her dress. Up? So that they plump and push together, or slung down and temptingly open at the neck. Some problem. I'm more enamoured with myself, must have another look, want to feel the pearl of my cheekbone, the whitefish flick of my drowsy lids. When I am expecting something like the texture of magnolias, I look up to the mirrored ceiling, and there, with a cat's intensity, staring down, is a terrible face, a caked and stretched, a pockmarked face, and it is me.

Place de l'Ancienne Boucherie

Plate glass window, lit up inside, steps out into the night, taking laundry blue walls with it, taking bunny baby shoes walking on a slender silver chain. Cumulus clouds pad the two soft hills. The window blows big soap bubbles. Each holds one hair and a tuft of lint. Fish eyes swim in search of bottles to bend around. Tumble and fluff your mohair till it's pink and purrs. The window asserts the room it is, *Self-Laverie.* Tomorrow's daylight stamped on the middle of midnight custard trails, where couples are smooth and caramel. Face to face they blend. Leg to leg they lean upon — Wet and moony cobbles, until *that* window, sends its postcard SKY to the shutter wall, roof and growl, of this dark *quartier.*

Deposit

Animal fiber, meaty, all thoughts turned out like tummy, like
custard from its shell. Stare. With the eye of belly. Butterfat.
Without a mouth to speak of— Eat, eat everything in sight, until
you're sightless, until you've swallowed yourself whole. Button-hole
in a mountain. Sounds like bear, bear lugging her late fall weight.
Ready to sleep. Ready to roll her mountain over and lie real round
like dirt. Moraine. Deposit yourself. Settle yourself down. While
the ice moves on the grass grows over. Lie still on your side and
rest, half dream, half wonder, why every night there is this obsessive
hunger— Tongue on the brain. The sleep of hibernation dreams
baby bears suckling up and down— How the first warm cream
shoots into each mouth, the pushing paws, their wanting to be
cuddled— All desire to roll on Mama, roll over brother and sister
fur and drink after drink at the warm round fountain, being held
to the spout without a thought. Soon. The first red berry each one
will taste, the sniff of new air snapped under the nose, after the
thin grey atmosphere of the cave. Now is the time for patience,
sleep, for soon they will sip from your heavy side, then slender and
rising you'll step from the ground that held you.

The Recipe

We have to catch ten shadow ponies to fulfill the recipe. They're very hard to hold in herd. Their skins come loose. We chase them up the corridor, secure them in the valley. Now back to the cook, dragging the ponies' shadows like ten suits slung on hangers. They are not willing. Will it ruin the taste, or make it more exciting? The entrance that we came by is now closing. We must dive through the exit hole, slide down the path on our now nude bellies. The rumor is passed back one by one that the last woman in line has a sensualist's history. I must be her. There's only one man behind me, groping my shoulder and whispering, Beautiful, beautiful bones. I hear the clatter behind, while he says he wants to turn us over— To the skeletons. I'm falling for it feels so good, him pushing me along this slippery alley. Yes I suppose I've had a sensualist's history, even when I was tiny: That warm snug cloth then squishing out sponged warm and smoothed with powder. I initiated many a youngster into the joys of the bedroom trailer where zucchini played its part. Perhaps I let myself go too many times, almost coming up too late, but the more I learned to love the more life thickened like a sauce, the sauce of the novel I might be writing. I've come to love with the suction of jello stuck down on a plate. How I have jiggled. Figures split like amoebas in my arms, two of the same and better. Yet now his words of sleek and shining skeletons have me almost convinced that the ultimate sexual thrill is to be boiled and served sloshing. This feeling wraps around me like an odor. His words stir up sensations deep inside me. It must be worth it, I decide, until I turn and see those bones, jiggering in lust and inescapable misery.

Mating Melody

As usual I'm dipping about in the water, going under more often than skimming along on top. He appears by the edge to trumpet up, Hi Chick. I go, Cheep cheep, and descend with the thought — What talk, where does this chap come from. Hey, I say to the hair there, do you want to see what I found on the bottom? I spill out of the water like Lake Upside Down, there by his side quite drenched yet not quenched entirely. I grab his waist and handle him very well with, Hang over, I'll hold you. He looks and I laugh, let him splash, a trick to get him into my element, that young elephant. Being gay as the day, I dive after to pinch this or that, when he isn't looking, can't see me coming, but he grows serious all wet yet. What did you expect, I cheep then check out down under, then up with my legs held around his, wanting to ride or do the trunk straddle, How about it? He looks confused, so I get a good breath for a long hold, but as I push off to go mud deep, he grabs my ankle and moves his grip right onto my fin and all over. I turn turtle, and he gets going now splashing and romping — It must be his first time in water. He takes me by surprise, with a slippery scale unequalled in air and we do it like boats when they sink as they float — Our motors have smooth round propellers.

Suckle Sex

Huge hungry horse lips close over my breast and pull. I watch in astonishment— How does it know not to eat me up? Then Luna the cat climbs to feed. Her lily-spike incisors could puncture, her kneading feet could claw, but it doesn't hurt— She is teaching me how and what I will do. Relax. Give in. Give way to the temple on the tit, the little hut of flesh that stands and sings for the letting down of milk. A system of blue-veined rivers runs uphill, to this well, to this sort of source. How nice to let the body offer on its own, first comfort. My animal man and I are learning a new way, concave convex, pregnant as sensuously full. My breasts before lay dormant, occasionally cozy as sand dune, but now irrigation makes good the soil, firms up my juicy hillocks, which want soft squeeze and so much attention, so much more a part of the full bodily tension to peak and release in swells. A part of the wave hard hump tidal zing that floats the body to a tumble. The rumble and subsiding. Then again— waters run inland run wild through fern shelter and low hanging coils, a jungle for the wet mouth that twirls out of line into circles, that goes for the neck meat, the lover's tunnel, his prick full-fleshed and blood-long, into my mouth, me squirming delightful. I want him to come in, come on in and be welcome. His weight— Want his body, I want to be ground with that circular motion, the grip rock and holding, want to live out the dream of the cat heat, how she raises her raw butt for relief for the come on, and enter mine too, backdoors, my ass in the air, my claws in the feather pillow, for the carving of the groove, the smooth sink, the pink meat pounding, till all is contentment. When I say I am feeling more mammal, I don't mean a cow to responses, but a milked and contented cow-feel might not be a bad one to have now and again. Contentment of every cell I say, as mud is relaxed, and the slow awakening when nothing calls— Then sun snuggles up and around you. The dream is persuaded to surface, like the enormous one-layer cake that rose up in the backseat, suspended in a liquid like jello. We bite right into the energy cookie, that first cake, placenta, our round and tummy baked creation. All enjoy their joy one way or another— Frog thumbs in armpits, cat teeth in cat neck, plunging in for both to swim in whatever way they ever imagined.

Going Out

Have you ever asked your husband, Honey, can I go on a date tonight? If you try, better not ask in that tone of voice. Better not ask. My husband and mother are talking, just out of view. My boyfriend kisses me with a tender teenage mouth and someone sees, someone is shocked to say the least. My husband and mother are sharing a cigarette, sharing opinions on my problem. My boyfriend suggests, Why don't we say we're going to the movies. But that sounds like a story. My mother is telling my husband how much she likes his style, his way with words. We enter dressed for a serious occasion. My husband smiles at my mother, Looks like youngsters asking permission. We sit down together, ready to explain our case. I rest my hand on his kneecap, liking the feel of his pants *and* his kneecap. Did you ever play football? My mother starts acting like a mother— Now, when will you be home what car are you taking? I look in my pocket but only find small change. This is as awkward as it ever was. She wants to know, When will the scout meeting begin and when will it be over answer me correctly. He has to tell her, my hand in his hand, It isn't a meeting, it's a— Date.

Suspicion

Prayer dog puppies are big warm dogs. Prayer dog puppies come out of the heat. They shed heat, padding through the garden with raccoon noses. Weird lookers. Well, it's nicer to be buried in heat than buried in cold. The infant graveyard lies on the other side of the mountain. Stones and bones all buried in deepest snow. Is it a comfort? All that big weight? Maybe they aren't so chilly, all in a row. Maybe they're just like— Completely asleep. I go to hug the prayer dog puppies, but being psychic— Slam the door shut just in time. Their tongues on the window encourage more raw beef in the salad. *No siree.* Enough raw beef in the salad already. Don't slobber. Everyone trying to get into my house today. First it was those prayer dogs, and now a crazy baby crawling up the stairs. It wants *in* so bad I don't think it's human. Those dogs are familiars. NO, can't let crazy babies in the house either. Now's when I go to find the stuffed glove to paint the highchair black, and find the prayer dog puppies mewing in the heat. I'm the only one home. Can't open the lock go out, because I'll have to come back maybe Find someone, snuck in the closet, but then, I feel like there might just BE someone in the house right now. In fact I don't feel safe. I'm psychic. Hear a creak. SEE, what did I tell you. My heart grabs all the blood in my body, ears enormous. Inward eye creeps a feel around the corner says, BOLT, unless you want to be Hacked, unless you want to be joints and limbs floating in the bathtub, for those prayer dogs to bury for that crazy to cry over a lost mama. But if I take to the streets— I can't go out like this. They'll be all over me. You've heard about this area, No? Well it's just not safe. I don't know where is. Maybe under that snow. Maybe way down below.

Saint Sanity

I'm sick, really disgusted, by the sight of all the fish in the refrigerator. They don't look like normal fish at all. My husband has been buying quite a lot of them lately, but he never gets around to cooking. I'll be damned if I'll touch those slimy— God, they're still twitching and blinking— Normal fish don't do that. I hear his girlfriend enter. I can hear them begin immediately, fawning and pawing and purring all over. I've just about had enough of it, sitting here making jelly cracker sandwiches with their voices on the radio. He calls it part of his job. It starts creeping over me, into every organ— Black dye curls through my veins— My teeth crack current jelly. Something in my spine is busted, something leaks and drips from my hands. I can't. I don't want to pull myself out of it this time. I'll wait in the courtyard where it's cool and quiet. Finally she comes to me, pleading with a silent coo, Have to get you out of here. It's getting late. She is dressed for the ride. She is dressed all in blue. I hold up cracker after cracker of jelly sandwich, Would you like one? She steps back, afraid of me, as if *I'm* dangerous, not my husband who's handing me a saber. I'm prepared, sitting cross-legged on the courtyard floor. I pull the blade out of its curved sheath, holding the point toward my empty stomach, but I see up above, in the lit window, a man with a crossbow ready to get me, ready to finish me off, and there on the other side is another. They are both taking aim. This takes the dignity out of my act. Seeing them there ready for murder makes me proud and self-saving. The official pats a pile of letters. He wants to get to the bottom of this incident, but my husband has no answer. He sits down to dinner. I'm eating simply, until I see that other coming toward our table, the one I desire. He sits down beside his sister at the far end. I watch the way he takes his napkin, the way he pours their water. My husband doesn't look up from his food but has a comment, Satisfied? Too bad he didn't sit next to you! I tell him firmly under my breath, Shut your mouth, or better yet— Eat your god damned fish.

Post Date

I'm conscious of my haircut. Will he like me this way? I've got my doubts since the *concierge* insists on calling me *Monsieur*. I'm staying at the cheapest hotel in Paris, where the customers are all sneaking a quickie with their heart's desire. Two women in my room are making sharp snap kisses. I pull the covers over my face, Go ahead, I'm not looking. He wants to know if I chose this place on purpose, because this is where he slept with his own sister. I try to lead him up the stairs, but does he follow? Does he change his mind? We kiss on the landing. He digs his way into me. I remember that. Why does it always feel so good making me lonely later. I ask him about the woman in his past, and he describes her, just the way I knew he would, with that look in his eyes. His eyes almost watch her turn over. I tell him, I always meant to be faithful, but when I saw you on the *métro* with that head of hair and soft blue scarf, when our eyes connected, I turned inside out like a pocket in your pants. The engine stopped the ride with me upside down— My hair falling downward, my change and direction all fell from my head. Please hold me. He puts his hand there. He gets close, almost unbearably close. He likes me hanging upside down like this. It gives him the power of gravity. Now he asks, so enchanting, such a sweet way, yet precisely like a scalpel, Why do you want a younger man? I can't remember the answer. Do I have to have an answer? I lose him in the house. I find him on a country road, writing a fat letter— I love you, I've been a fool. The one he never sent.

Hotel Comfort

When you first check in, the man behind the counter takes your hand. He says that if he feels it, he can tell how good you are in bed. He rubs your hand, if you let him, if you like to have your fortune read, with a sensuous sweet country massage, sweetness by Rudy. The waiters in this hotel get closer than you might think necessary, but you will grow accustomed, even look forward to their available air in the lobby. It's all part of the package deal. Needless to say this hotel is always crowded, so book way in advance especially during the ski season. Everyone closes an afternoon affair with, We'll have to *wedel* together like this more often. Now that you know, you won't have to believe him. If you happen to ask at the desk, What's the name of that run, the one that cuts down across the others like a cat walk? I can already tell you, it's called— Cheating. It's at the bottom of that run that I get caught beneath an avalanche. I can actually hear the *après-ski* folk, how they walk and talk with their cocktails above me. It's a suffocating feeling. I struggle to free myself with such upward adrenalin, that they have to bring me down in a balloon basket manned by my father, who always descends in flying colors, especially when he has a chance to entertain the clientele. When we hit ground outside the lobby, a whole class of Swiss school children want a ride. They look creepy to me, like little albino men in young bodies, ash white hair, Tyrolean outfits. My father acts just like himself, making a big deal out of nothing, making a short trip a cause for mounting excitement, always make it a party if you can. He can. I'm perfectly willing to let the whole mob take my place in the balloon basket. Besides, I'm this evening's entertainment. The guests of the hotel each take turns making home away from home movies, and it's funny watching so-an-so make sudden motions for the roving camera, the squeals of disbelief, *I* don't look like that, do I? Yes, that's me in the bathing pool, the water so clear, nothing is hidden, everything is visible. There I am looking up at the camera from below the water surface, and now we have myself turning, as I pretend to be the axis of a liquid world. And on our right— Hey, someone shouts from the audience— Look at that beautiful body! Wouldn't you know it's my father. He thinks I look just like him.

Those Who Belong Together

He's getting married to her again, and this time there seems to
be nothing I can do about it. Can't stop it now. The words are
said it's over. That part of it anyway. They are not what you'd call,
how do you put it— Madly in love with each other, but they are
successful at acting out long looks of affection. The congregation
says, Believable, and they pass the test. I'm waiting outside in the
telephone booth as they make their archway exit, slipping through
the gates of the limousine, but he crawls over the seat and out the
other side to join me in the phone booth. What have you brought
for a wedding present this time, he asks? I nod to the package,
and he turns it over carefully, as if handling the shoe from his dead
sister's foot. If it hadn't been for that accident, he'd never be in
this position. Close quarters for conversation, much less a recep-
tion. He lets the string and paper fall to the floor and the box springs
into action, sprouting with the first contact of oxygen. He pulls
the grass-stuffed box apart, and out stands an egg, a big cerebral
egg, engraved with the markings of a black brain. It's throbbing.
I lift his hand, place the egg snugly between his legs. What? he
asks, as if he hadn't heard right? Your first born, I said. I feel
cramped by my position in the telephone booth. The air between
us is going fast, so I fold open the door and she's there waiting
with a dime in her palm but she hasn't heard a thing. My ap-
pearance replaces her need to make a phone call. She wants me
to come and see her wedding presents. Her favorite is this card-
board construction, shiny, bright pink cardboard. She demonstrates
as she explains that it comes in six pieces and can change from
bed to ironing board to kitchen cabinet. I pretend to be amused,
but can't help despising this projected pink decor and the obvious
potted plants and pineapples that will go with it. She forgets about
me and acts like a greedy kid the afternoon after— How many,
how good, before the lack of attention sets in— How bored bor-
ing, grate grating, irked irksome, being married, married to you,
you pouch of potatoes. But for the moment she's completely ab-
sorbed and doesn't see me run down the slope to the waterfront
where he's turning in frustration like an insomniac on his king-
size beach towel. I take his head in my hands and rub the pound-
ing temples. What have I done, he says, the whole thing was half

28

an act, half a matter of convenience. I'm not even ravenous for her. It's as if I made use of a free ticket to some place I never wanted to go. But you're back now, I answer. When the kiss comes to us, lightly, delicately at first, then with energetic hunger, all those half-hearted promises slip away, through somebody else's fingers. Our union goes unspoken, but we're both relieved. He brushes his thick tipped lashes and shakes the sand from my hair, then sits up alert. The waves are lunging. Not that our consummation had anything to do with it. Nature isn't out to blame anyone in particular. It just has to get up and grunt once in a while like you or I do. We make for the path, secure the door to our beach shanty, then settle down as if we'd lived here for ages. He is in the kitchen cooking chops, while I sit at my desk recording the days events, when four members of the wedding party barge through the door. They don't notice that we aren't the original couple. They are simply embarrassed— How can he enjoy cooking while I relax in my nightgown and slippers. I mean really, on our wedding night, coming to complain about the rising cost of food being equal to the rising of the surf, I call that ignorance. I say to myself in a ho-hum tone of voice, If you ignore them, they'll go away. And sure enough, when I turn back to my massive notebook, they all disappear.

Shut Down Shut Down Twice

As a man, he has been here at home, talking with my husband for some time. He assumes the shape of an old lost lover. Can I make you a milk shake? Sure. Everything's in it but the shake. When he scratches himself, I see that the rings are gone. I want to please but lecture him with his own old lecture, not even liking the sound of his voice. Next, he searches through the sheets on the bed. He has the top sheet over his shoulders and says, I am lost, I am really lost. Sure. But do I want to find him. As a woman, I look in her eyes. It's ready to go love from my side, though she is cool with contempt for me. I must explain to her my egg salad sliced thin with mayonnaise. Don't you know the feeling? How I once felt for him— Now here she is again. But she dismisses me, Control yourself. A boy comes and holds my hand. I'm afraid to look at him in case he's too ugly. I can sense that he is very ugly. Why else would he want to hold my hand. I look. I'm your equal now, he says. I run, jump the tennis fence, I run on and on until the doors begin to open— A closet door pulled open to another door a closet door pulled open to another to a corridor, where I reach her room. She is busy, but I have brought a present. She accepts, What is it. These words, I blubber, I Love You! She says, cut-the-crap-like, YOU DO NOT. I'm razed dazed amazed at myself as I grab her round face her round black hair and squeeze out, When you are no longer younger, when no one thinks that you're so hot, if it takes forever I will wait for you. Well I won't look, she answers. Now out of here!

What You Eat

She tells me that he's the most beautiful boy she's ever seen. I believe her. It is clear that her house is covered with snow, as are the homes of all of the others, who have seen his mane of thick blond hair. He is the lion, the young lion, unaware of the strength he will soon possess. I lie back in the field of high grass and bluebells, aching with passionate postures. He is drawn to me. I say, Put your hands on my shoulders, lean down and kiss me. It's successful. You just have to be direct and simple. In the car he asks me my sign, but already, Wait, he knows, It's fire. I've never known anyone like you, he says. I agree. No, I mean the way you burn, it's obvious. I blush. That's not typical. He pulls the car up beside her. She has become gigantic. Envy? Her skin has stretched to the limit, breasts netted with blue-black veins, full as possible, tight. We follow the lines of her breasts pointing to the street market packed with people. Someone screams, I have to buy a carrot! Here is the picture I made, torn down the middle, but pasted back together in my journal. It shows people holding up chicken eggs. The eggs are bigger than they are. The eggs remind him of marriage. I didn't bring it up. He is not to be stopped though. He says, I think the repetition might make sex taste like hamburger. He can't bear the thought of me, his Laurie, as plain old hamburger. I smile at him, as if I know better— This is what does it *this,* I waggle a carrot. Just look in my eyes. He does, feeling almost unbearably silly. It's a puddle warm feeling of putty in his nuts. He smiles at himself, tries not to show it, then tumbles me down, playful but growling— Nice, those nips on the neck that could hurt.

Musical News
(1970–1978)

Wish for Water

We rise to comb the fine mist from our hair—
Roll down to shore, this hour of the morning.
Sunrise then, the rite begins with wonder—
The couple turns— It's over. We
come alive laughing. Champagne bubbles in the air.
A wonderful way to go up the stem.
The llama says good morning
to his breakfast of hydrangeas.
We are all in a circle— The water dances
round our legs. The llama milks the flowers.
We extend our hands to kiss and be good friends
and love each other daily. We will mend the sky
we will heal each other. Lift off
like leaves into everything feels so good.
Kick up! This is the morning
of the wedding sliding by.
                    Light
          on the grass
                    the waves are—
                              flashing.
She sees how it should happen. She will
not disappoint them.
                    But her bed now
this lake, is wet with, her hair
is washed back, and her ears are full
of tears.
The ache that takes over her body
hurts, like glaciers giving up
to the change, the melt
gives way to water.
                    She floats—
                              He floats
          away.

She holds him over and over
prolonging the dream she wakes from
guilty with feelings.

Crush them.
No—
Nurture them.
They will be your only children.

Holding onto the fact
of her new life is slippery, as the wet rail fence
she'd cross, going off
alone through the wet fields
away from it all.
The high grass swims.
The spider dew could buoy her, but threads
the web, is easily torn, and every song
sounds sad to her.

The sweet champagne has made her cry.
The dance is slow
and graceful, hands in a circle
so soon broken, makes her cry.

They throw her tissue
paper hearts, which flutter in the air. Her heart
would land
and melt there at their feet.
But she's the bride—
They both step in. She's sailing
the water like the body of her groom
is dying in her sail like a weak wind.
She would have the sail in rags, old
banners, her body
thrown to the waves.

She does not look at the man beside her, owned
but down for her lover, somewhere in the water.
She will sink to him.
The songs they sing
from the shore fall over
her head like a huge sail tipping.
Her breath, held back
makes the heart go faster.
Her gown, spreads out, like an open rose—
His love, dark water

rushing around her
carries her down
to home.
Where his hands will rest upon hers.

Deserted

When I cross the field, the bulls stand up
                in their orchard
and watch me.
           Keeping their tongues
                    still in their mouths.
The calves come near, when I crouch
           in the grass, and call to them.
Their coats are creamy.
              I just want to touch
one of them.
           But when I step forward they
tumble-back-upon-each-other.

This farm seems deserted
             but the pigs are trotting.
I never knew a pig could
             move so fast.
The wheat just beginning
             in cool green thrashes—
The day given over
             like a newborn thing
        passed
             hand to hand.
Everything beginning
             and my heart goes with it
       until I think of him.

A bull scrubs his neck against the trunk of a tree.
I too would nip the blossoms
fill my mouth with that delicate odor.

I think the man who's left this place
           waits somewhere else
for the fattening.
             Until he can gather
        all of the apples

                              press them
for what they're worth.

No man now, is around, I assure them.

                    Only you in your pastures
watch a woman shake the boughs
for the blossoms
                         to fall
                                   in her hair.
Only you
              her her laugh
                         and then cry
like a rooster.
Only you hear her testify.

July

Grandmother
to read from you
how one life was not enough
for everything you felt for him
it moved these twenty years
into your gathering, as if you were a golden poppy
curling shut.
And I want to be there
inside with you, to fight
that crawling illness, which creeps
into your precious organs, that still love back
that still remember so concisely
giving hope that I
can make it too.
And I come
down from your stem
into your roots and see
there is still much life here.
For it's the spirit, not the blood
that finally counts, when you leave off measuring
look past waiting —
Gramma
the insides of your curling flower
are the softest. From many rains
on country fields you've come into a thousand
golden flowers bending up the slope.
We gallop our horses through them. We ride
for that brown wood fence.

Retired Farmer's Prayer

Now it's my time to go
to go back where I came from.
Time to pack the trap, pet the barn cats
set the hoes in their places.
But don't run my eyes
over all those years— Yeah.
cryin' like a baby
leave the door
swing.

Convince myself
about the quiet of the pine bed.
Convince myself
about the parting of the stream.
But earth is sand
this side of the river
and I long for the cheeks of my goats oh God
and I pace this trailer.

For who'll be coming
to chew the Copenhagen
gnaw the fat cut the bacon
this winter when the afternoons go dark
when the horses no longer look up
steaming in their stalls, waiting to be fed
and the cribbage pegs stay in their holes
Dear Lord and the brew in its jug.

My hands fold together, late at night
prayer wings hold my head. Why
did I dream of the forest for so long
when the fields are between these palms of mine
when my animals licked these wrists.

Eyes of the Garden

We have come home here
to be revived by the balm of greenwood and grasses
and the gathering hours in the garden
where feet sink into black earth
and tomatoes are picked sun warmed, and in the mouth
still warm, where zucchini hair prickles
when snapped from the vine
and the swelling bust of summer squash
are arranged in a basket with zinnias.

We come back to this wicker basket to be born again
from the warm potted smell of the greenhouse
into the pace of farmers.
Our days spread out like fields to be grazed
slowly in this August heat.
And yet we are still waiting. Expectation
is a thin honey on our skin.
It's something like the storm's approach
a tense-green violet
over the stillness of the water's teal.

We have come back to be cleansed from distance
from speed and the people we passed like mere items
in too many approaches and quick departures.
Relief lies like a wound at the bottom of the lake
where we cry beneath dark waves
for the ache of coming
and the ache of going away again.

Still nourished by communion of summer
the long arms of cousins, the flush on a sister's face
the hair of my brother, holding on to them for survival.
Back to the oldest woman
who has kept us together like memory.
And now to sit with her and hold her hand
while she diminishes, gazing.

Her skin is of the delicate pansy
her odor of fading roses.
But her eyes are delphinium, blue without reserve
so sure of their love, so clear against the slur of days.
And when she attaches them to us, we see the ache for living
in them, that her love has the strength
of shoots breaking ground, again and again.
And now we have come to watch the flower drop
so slowly from her hand
catching that star to continue.
And though she is quiet now
I know that her eyes are speaking—
Speaking with the voice of the whole garden.

The Woman Who's Trapped Beneath
the Seasons

She walks away— from the house
holding onto her first child
big in the belly
knowing her husband
is taking another woman.

The sky presses down
on her weight.

She sees— smashed in the fields
good melons
a farmer, down on his knees
over ripped vines
his hands heavy on the ground.

The Woman with Love Child

As we locked bodies and gripped for the gateway
I knew
someone burst into being
an angel out of nothing
and I carried him high
through those nine month miles, despite their questions
and I sang to the wet winds
that took away the father he would never know
but it didn't seem to matter.
He swam out of my womb a love child
smooth as a swan
black as a swan
and when he smiled for the first time, my heart
beat its heavy wings
until the air stirred around us.
And when the government voice
said bastard, state, belongings —
We flew, we flew.

The Unmarried Woman Giving Her
Child Up for Adoption

I decided to do it this way from the very beginning.
Once I knew
I stuck to that
though as he got bigger I felt him inside *so strong.*

I know I did best
for both of us —
A good home, a family
the name that I chose as he was born —
A rush of energy swept over me
passed through the cord
into his being and I felt radiant
relieved.
They said, Boy, but I kept my eyes
shut, so that I would never see him.

Yet as I left that city, three years later
I thought I heard
his voice so terribly sad saying —
Don't leave me, I don't want you to go.

The Woman Who Went Along With It

It's not the right time for either of us.
She knows that's true but
is that the reason.
She places his hand on her swelling and later alone she
cries through her teeth.
His refusal to be the father
seems so distant, unbelievable as
cold stars stabbed
into somebody else's heaven.
He says he'll find the doctor
drive them there and pay.
Afterwards her eyes, scraped bare
are those twin frozen stars
which he looks away from.

The Woman Who Chose Abortion

I panicked when my period didn't come.
Pictured it as a thing
taking hold
like a leech
on a leg, fat with my blood.

The doctor with his mean eyes
and accusations
saying that he'd fix me
this time
and the nurse's invisible chanting
making sure I saw the fetus
in its see-through plastic tub —
Dirty scissors and the sheet
some other woman's
blood I've got my reasons —
A life to heal and live on.

The Woman Whose Child Is Born Dead

I was working so hard—
Labor was long wasn't coming the doctor
didn't know
couldn't feel it until
that expression on his face
unwrapping the cord.

Just minutes before inside
we heard the heartbeat *booming* over the monitor.
The pediatrician worked and *worked*
over the body for half an hour
trying to make her *breathe*
and Jerry and I were praying
with the priest who had come with the holy water.
Then the doctor just gave up
stood there and said—
I'm sorry.

The hardest part was coming home
thinking, maybe I didn't want her
bad enough.
No the hardest part was
telling everybody.

The Woman with Too Many
Children Already

Is truly in a shoe
tied up tied down expecting
another she grabs the toddler
by the shirt back
balancing baby on her square hip
slicing with one hand the evening
supper again
again attention sprawls
in every direction she calls to stop
that Daddy's gonna hear about
their mouths the constant
question what
to put into them—
Answers, tries
to fill demands
but needs an hour a long
vacation.
She's not that basket
of bread replenished
not even recharged at the dinner hour
but eats in jerks and angry
can't
though when she sees those
fighting brothers
collapsed in bed their arms
around each other
sleeping links them
all she feels
it must be worth it.

The Woman Who Takes Care of
Other People's Children

She loves the son as her own, but has to keep
her distance when Mother comes into the room.
She would offer her breast
if he were hers, but instead
she holds his naked body in her bare arms
for that completeness.
She knows how to make quiet
how to bring his smile to the surface.
She gives and gives and stays
in the background.
She's not sure how she should feel
but she too breaks down
when he leaves home for good.

And even as a man, he wonders —
Whose arms, that comfort.
Until out of the reservoir
the bottomless reservoir at midnight cradled
on his death bed
he calls for his mother and sees
one face
and longs for another's
dense black hair.

Dear Helen

I'd like to see the marriage you imagine possible— Autumn bleeding everywhere, out of the opening in the forest where I'd follow, the trail of your dress to the vows said. Then *bells* of air. Mountains of air. Vows you have in your texture already taken. Or will you trash it all. Will his doubts undo? I want you to be happiest, like a parent might, present you with running water for your homemade house, seeing how you're fresh to this union. As crushed pine sends its flavor up, we watch the watercrash. Looking down you say, *This is where he first told me.* I am only a cousin wanting the best for you, or secretly Greedy common typically Wanting you to marry like Me have a child like Me, so we can be more one in day and expectation. I could ring the copper bowl, write a lyric for the ritual of the first wed evening, but *I'm* not the man with the words stuck in his thought box, in the contrary custom, in the cinderstove under the stript wallpaper the barewood the asking. And what if he decides No. What then? And what if he decides Yes. What then.

Dear Geoff

Thirteen days without you, and yet I am not without you. You are at ease inside me, like a perfect organ, pumping away. I haven't had one jealous thought, or worried too much about it. You say this week you're more aware of my absence, like— What to do about dinner. In retrospect, I'm mildly offended, but realize how much we do reflect and double each other's world, nonsense and humor. This lake air is good for me though and you've stopped smoking. More bed to fill, diagonal, but I'm coming to trust and think I could even live with myself. No wonder you miss me No? I'll thrill to find your searching face, four hours non-stop to Berkeley. Seven years non-stop, our brains and our bodies, nudging each other, and yet I feel the wings of a future rushing through ozone not knowing where, till the final explosion slaps one of us down— Even then, no stopping the beat for the other— No stopping the changing altered years.

Dear Lyle

Tonight I feel your absence. Haunting, echo, hollow. The *whoop* of owls lovemaking surrounds the black oak trees. Reverberations of the moon and her bellow song, if she had one, she'd sing for you, and I can be glad for you, thinking of the breathless doe that will come to your window, and the buck that will press the shape of his sleep in the high grass— Silence, that best comforter, when you're comfortable in your own skin, in your northwoods trailer, the electric finally in and no one getting you up at the wrong hour or telling you how to do it. Retiring from these parts, that have grown too many cars too much business. Bad air, bruises. But good things too have grown here, and we have eaten from the hand of your labor. The early morning dew-thick hour, the sopping shoes, the cold bent hand that offers. We take. You go. Like the stars go.

Dear Laura

I know you, like nobody knows you, and that is a load. How you twist and thrive on extreme, with the romantic swoon of the home dweller, whiplashed on violence contained, causing your anger. Look out— Open the window. It's the quiet hour of the cat. See, it drops into the garden. How you want to absorb that singleness. How you want to cry in the movies, and take, as well as be taken. O yes, and the world must adore you, though your effort be purely selective, your offering small. My God there is room for improvement! And I don't only mean that the head is too strong for identical internal likeness and the hair is impossible. For myself now I'd like to repeat— *No matter what* (expose your flower, let it be touched) *I can go on.* So I tell you, with the darling hurt heart of a pony, barbed and shaken, that sometimes you can not get out, except to retreat, into the silence that's speaking.

Dear Stan

He asked me, as we lay back on the lawnchairs, as he twisted
another lemon into another iced vodka, if you were *the best*, or simply
my favorite, and why. Favorite, I had to admit, though best had
been my original statement. *But why*, he asked. *Because*, I said,
because— I do not know. I tried to think of what makes molten
rock erupt through a vertical, why lava is forced to muscle the air
that it flies through, what makes one engine unify. I imagine when
certain lips part, a moon rides around on a river, and the trees
the heavenly trees combine. Thrill tipped on the tongue, and how
it chunks into the target, and how it *arrives* at the moment. Clear
on the rim the ringing. I lay your good book down, disturbed by
my love for these poems. Because? I can not say. Because, I said,
he *knows*.

Dear Jill

I have probably written you more than any other person on this earth. It hurts me to think of our friendship as anything less than immortal. (Oh, now I've embarrassed the reader.) But how can I tell them that what we have shared just isn't that common a thing. We've been on the road with the roof down, climbed for the hill scooping up the berries, finding the righteous, almost. Until Otis came on the radio, and you said, *Don't cry, you'll be with him, forever now.* And I wrote you (quite D. H. Lawrence), that I also needed a female companion of equal importance in another sphere. You know I will always be there for you, that my lines will continue to travel the distance. It's an *arc-en-ciel* that configuration — our pots of gold spring forth. You are probably the one person in this world, who I will remain at peace with.

Dear Kate

I was told today. Today the trees tolled. Today I went in. Your way today Kate. Today gone to memory. Kate I heard you today. Today I got down. All the trees told me nothing, of what it is not to *see* today Kate. If I could reach my hand in, under the skin of today, I would stroke the long ribbon of your spine today Kate. I would guard you the perimeter of your privacy. I would needle the dark with your talk today Kate. I would moisten the music, as noontime rings. All the sandstone doors would swing open today. I would haul in the sky, and allow for you Kate. I was told I was told. I am listening Kate.

Pavane for the Passing of a Child

after the music of Ravel

Possible
that I lift this hand
feel a weight I've never felt there.
Possible
I hold this weight
collapsed and sunk and tamed now
feel a flesh so warm gone under
that will not home.
I give her back
for whom I sang
I sing no longer.

Possible
my arms surround
will lay her down this last time
not return —
There was no claiming her
but in this taming of her.
I give her up I hold her here
all that is left to me.
I hold I can not
give her up —
I lay her down.
My arms fold over.

And then she took the child
and then she laid the child to rest
and then she laid the cover
on the child, and then she closed her heart.
And it tore over her —
She turned away to face it
and in the door the light came in
and made a breakfast of her.
It spread all over her.
It sucked and made a vacant space there.

Where there had been a child—
A child no longer.
It sucked her fill.
She let the sobs come
take her gut and wrench
the place of blood
where she had spilled and grown and swollen
where she had borne and held and given
what had been pulled from her
what had been torn
was taken.
What had been chance and breath
what had been closer than
her mouth her hope her plea and cry
was aching.

She stood there in the sun
and it disgraced her.

The plate
the cup
the dress the bed and book
turned over.
The toy the finger smudge
the corner
folded.

If sea could tear and water hold a stone
she'd sink there.
Was told
to let her go—
It was no good—
The light crashed through her.
She meant to force it
swell up and take her too
but something stopped inside
marked off and framed her.
Before, there was a lingering
and now an outline
a separation.
She was retreating.
The force welled up—

She stopped.
She gave it back.
Refused to nurse it.

The light came on
came on and planted her.
She felt nothing.
The sun rose up
and smeared itself all over her.
But she felt nothing.
The man who stood behind
and placed his hands upon her shoulders—
She felt nothing.
She felt nothing.
The sky that morning flatter than she'd ever known it.

And then she took the child
and then she laid the child to rest
and then she laid the cover
on the child
and then she closed her heart.
And when she turned away
it made a breakfast of her.
It sucked, and made a vacant space inside her.
Where there had been a child
a child no longer.
The blood place wrenched
where she had spilled
where she had born and held
what had been torn
was taken.
What had been breath
her mouth her hope and plea
was aching.

The plate the cup
the dress the bed and book
turned over.
Held back and gone
her song was sung
the sod was heavy in her.
It could not cover.

Coming Clean

I can not believe
that I can believe what I'm hearing
when he decides to come clean.
When he hands me the secrets
he's been sharing with no friend.
Unstitching the cheat.

I'm a boat— I'm relieved for
we haven't allowed
such sincerity in ages.
But hold, he is going
to get it all
out now.

The more
recent is harder I am
one-eyed white
on my side not touching
down on *that happened?*
How could I
not *know?*
Didn't want to, even
with my did-you-demanding.
I've never known anyone
else, a fool.
No, not angry.
Nothing
anymore.

He admits, that even years ago
when our union first happened
I had something so ready so
overpowering— Dazed
I raced on my own consummation
containing him so well
he had no need to devour—
No flame burned there.

You mean you never
really had it
for me just
sort of
came over
and all the family function
for the dollar undermined
your wanting to give no reason to
given? You mean *she*
made you twist
to her every
little
gesture?

            I wonder
            if anyone
            if it
            will ever happen
            if someone
            will ever fall
            like that
            for me.

I want a Big Love
that could flare
for a nation. Want to *shine*
on this earth I would feed that fire everything.
Swan up in the flame and *spring* from the ashes.
I will not believe I have already spent it.
Look
right into my face
listen.
I never suspected. Truly
I trusted.
But you lied
into the lies and made some fine knot work.
For you gnarled up inside
so hard everything disgusted.
But you did it so smoothly that nothing showed through.
You are all clean now, you are washed with your telling.
But I am telling
you nothing.

And I am showing you
nothing.
Why
should I give you
the gift of my sadness.

Only in bed
alone later
only there
do I lava
and lie in
rumble my cry through
the sheet twist I tear off
my shirt strip the holds I am
Blasted do damage don't care
cut myself on it *see*
for I hate fuck you *shit* you
can't even make me
complete
anymore.

And wake up
in the morning
next to his body
not quite as familiar.
He in undisturbed sleeping.
Though the air, as it is in Berkeley after downpour
stands incredibly clear.

Outside, down the street— Sight
to the waters incredible.
The firs of Marin
are fuzzy, and visible.
The sharp, little sailboats
each so singular, Sunday—
Walking
with the baby
to nowhere.

Last Breath

When the petals of the plum tree
swirl up
     before my headlights
I turn the car downhill and drive.

Because I can't see
    the way the apple flower
    snows the air
the way the fever
of the plum
is brooding everywhere in Berkeley

I drive and I am driven.
Tightly smooth   and
forward in my black compartment.

Thinking things
that make me know   my
heart still beats.

Loving in a way
that will not get there.
So if I weep   behind this steering wheel

I say that it's ok
here in my privacy.

I can allow myself   one luxury.

Let it go now
as behind
the petals from the plum   turn brown
    and blow
down the dark driveway.

Goodnight Moon

I turn off all the lights
so that Clovis can see the moon.

The moon is full tonight.

(painfully so.

And I tell him that lovers kiss.

I could also say   that the callas

blooming   at the bottom of the steps

are white
and round
and vaginal

in the moonlight.

But the enormous stalks have swooned
and the flowers also
have laid their goose heads down
right onto the pavement.

Formal Feeling

The stars
are so distant

       and mute.

     Fierce
   is their quiet.

        Little
      is their light.

I too
am remote

    and do not speak now.

          My weakness
         is to write.

   When I should demand

       all absence
       inhabit me.

The moon   not a gong—
The stars   but reminders

      that nothing really pours
      out of the sky.

    Certainly
    your refusal
    to be here

       makes me write this

  and more
until even hope leaves me.

Memory

Yes
it is fine
the thought of your milky

man's mouth
over mine.

As I wake slowly

the cardinal sings.

With me here
on the high brass bed—
Over the green rug life no longer

seems to fear.
As I wake slowly
and Clovis calls.

We walk naked

mother & son
through the soft air
of the yellow hall.

Simply

As I walk out of the *La Belle*
the small town theater is at ease tonight.

Automobile weather
and the framed house lights

are balanced on the curved
shallows of the bay.

I do not know why it touches me
that the children are riding their bikes home

over the bridge water

under the street lamps.

The Fear

I was talking to Gloria on the phone
and just before I hung up   (I'd been so happy
just to hear her voice
a mutual effervescence (that's the word) when one can be
nearly mindless with a friend
a kind of *glee*
that meets along the wire and makes of sound
a ball of light
surrounding you both)
but just before I hung up
before good feeling left us
before the phone was hooked and silence resumed
I was enlarged by a body of fear
that rose like a hand to a jellied glove . . .

Which had nothing to do with Stephen
who had visited an hour earlier
and how I saw him through the door, so glad
because our eyes were equally pleased —
(as in sharing a secret
without having to speak it)   Immediately
he sensed the erotic after-image, yours —

>"Well!" he said.
>"Whatever's been happening to you —
>It must be good!"

And I laughed outrageously.
You know I want to laugh like that
all-the-time
and throw my head back
with a soft explosion of *pink*
behind my brain, the pillowing plunge point
where it gushes
up through the laughter to be alive!

But I am also
quite content

in the motion you
bring with you
as in the gentle rocking of boats
way out of bounds.

Kindness
equals the time it takes
to allow
a lulling. Tenderness
I'm not
ready to do without.

And then I hung up the phone.
Lay down on the sofa.
And read chapter four from Bergman's
Scenes from a Marriage.
Chapter of truth, of brute truth
laughable hate, and too bad
outrage, of boredom and considerate divorce
and how it never is
polite when you are honest — (Thank God
and fuck the considerate lies too) —
How one can not *believe* the signals
and even when it's signed
(the papers were not
the meaning anyway)
still married, or
never again, never again, never again, never again!

And it was so accurate
I felt a heavy burden of tiredness
and just lay there
and didn't do
anything for a while, with arms lapped over my chest
turned sideways
as in the motion of hugging my own breath —
I rested
and listened
to the filtered siphon of traffic passing
not asleep but in the semi-doze
of a traveler, walking alone at night
paused by a window, hearing the murmur of talk

behind glass in a warm room
wanting to be there.

But then as I lay
my body filled the glove again
and coolness rose . . .
Shadow-dread formed to fit me.
And I was taken up again
in the hands of a benevolent strangler
moving his choke to my wind gate
as if to seduce all oxygen
and no resistance there
just a slow accepted suffocation
coming down like an interminable dream
where I will know
absolute darkness
and the heart will hold
that box of blackness
will be resigned
will not have the courage to move
will not be the winner of will power
will in a sense give up
to the Inevitable
which is simply a choice not to choose!

Then I will loosen my fingers from the living
and your hair will fall out of my hands, your shoulder
skin will slip away
and your tongue will dissolve in my mouth
my mouth will be sand of no substance
until I have the unembraceable feeling of falling
and nothing will be there to stop it
but the hands will inhabit the darkness with me
and I won't be able to see them
and I won't be able to feel them when they touch me
and there won't be any light
not even on the edges of objects
and then I won't be able to breathe at all
and I won't really care about it
and I will simply stop breathing
and then no body will contain me.

Lost Dog

It is only the friendly presence of afterlife
who is guiding me down to the ocean
down through the sunlight to the fog still lovely
a wonderful place to go to the ocean
taking me down . . .

    I've been this way before —
    But never get there.
    Stopped by a change of dream —
    I've lost the record player.

Is that what marriage means?
    Now,
        I am the curly black dog with red bandana
    who does not know its master
    who will not hear its name.
    I am also the person calling —
    "Lincoln! Lincoln!" *(((come home*

It that what marriage means?
Divorce, a sturdy division.
The child, the fusion.
Is that what?

I took one babystep out
of monogamous apprehension
and I was drilled . . .
The machine gun mouth was held to my forehead
and it kicked out the brain's storehouse.

    Smoke of exploded emotions.
Then,
    I gathered my immediate cigarettes
    (this is the fog)
    thinking, OK, I could lose everything, and by myself
    sleep in the back of the Fiat.
But I didn't have anywhere to go as I got out.

Everyone looked so far away.
Even the onion soup and warm bread barely made the
          distance.
And I was the walking blob
looking at shoes
crying at her not-at-home doorstep.
Until I met Summer on the street . . .

   Oh the waves of grief in my friends' arms—
I do not have to ask them to hold me.

   Sometimes
   you just let go.
   Like Clovis with his 3 helium balloons
   which deliberately nudged the ceiling.
   But the greatest pleasure of all for him
   was to take them out, early in the morning—
   "When you get too cold, come back inside,"
   he said as he released them.
It that what marriage means?
   And the sky embraced them.

"But love," she said, over caffè latte in the Med
"has become so twisted with possession.
It's constancy you cling to.
Your happiness isn't a crime."

"For Christ's sake, I just don't want to be sat on.
I don't want to be pinned down with questions
or Told. Don't want the panic of guilt
when the phone rings
when I want to just come down to breakfast
and not be commented upon."

   Will I be the old woman
   who lived next door
   who leaned over the fence and told me—
   "I've been married now
   for fifty-five years . . .
   and always self-conscious with him."

We scare each other
into predictable performance:

74

Now you be the husband
and I be the wife.
You be the watchdog and protect us both.
You be the child, unite us.
You be the house that holds us.
Oh there be trouble in paradise.

So I finally made it to the Other's house
where I had no sense of belonging.
And he was the lump of no solution.
I was smart enough to kiss him goodnight
and get the hell out with my expectations.

I walked out of *that* door
and felt like the laser of light now
who had fucked around in the fog too long
and drove without thought for Cedar.
I was riding the rope called Desperate.
It was the sorrow of the severely weary.
And he met me under the hall light
and I laughed through my tears about finding two apartments
but how I didn't want to leave him.
And we kissed and I cried and said I was sorry
selfish *selfish* selfish.
The middle selfish
self-righteous.

Clovis, upstairs
in pajamas, sitting on the middle of the carpet—
"I didn't know where you Are."
And I picked him up
and lay down on his bed—
"You know I love you.
And I love Geoffie too.
And Lincoln too . . ."
"And *Nay-Nay?*"
"Yes, and Nay-Nay."
"Lincoln got hit by a car?"
"I hope not. Sleep, now sleep," kissing him
        on cheek's softest skin—
                        And yes
the meaning.
It has no beginning, middle or end.

Until Death, Do It

Who knows what jungle bird flies loose
to send its echoing recall
over the pine and poplar
of Lincoln Street towards Cedar
but at dusk I hear its inhaled sound
drawn back through a tunnel— *Three times*
the No Bird.

And in the middle of the night, no hour
who hears me? gulping on grief
having seen Clovis
dead in the dream, in a small wooden
plain pine coffin.

> He was lying in the open box, in his t-shirt, pale blues
> and I think he was still alive
> because when I took his hand, limp at the wrist
> and asked him where he was
> he said—
> > *'Far away.'*

Far away
in a voice that would make
huge canyons minuscule.

> And then Lyle the old farmer
> turned him over on his side
> so that he would be more comfortable
> and then his whole small body went tight as a wrench
> rigid and cold as aluminum.

I couldn't stop crying.
"Sit up, try to get in a different head," he suggested.
I did
sit up, kept sobbing
went to the bathroom, came back, under the sheets—
(Aware it was only a dream) cried harder.

Sleep baby. Sleep.
Down where the woodbines creep.

So peaceful, far away, the child
our fusion, lost—
My loss, I realized
because then I was angry, pleading— "Don't!
Doesn't this child have something *here* to accomplish!"
But then I knew my selfishness
holding him back or
then I whispered
                    "Fly— Fly into the arms of the light."

This morning, naturally normal.
This morning, he was naked and alive in bed with me as
        always.
Feet pushing under the covers.
I kissed his little shoulders.
And when he got out of bed
I saw his three year old body as Boy
before he went downstairs for banana
before he marched back up.
"Too much noise
coming up those stairs.
You woke up the puppy."
Tango.
And then I had to get up, and slowly
cheerios for breakfast, his new red plastic sandals
him holding the kitty-cat *Sofa*
reading her a book backwards.

        Dear Geoff,
        Would you really marry Laura all over again?
        Come to LA anytime. The sofa makes a nice bed.

And then to walk upstairs
and see the broken line of Christmas lights
plugged into the electrical socket.
Several bulbs just jagged glass
the crimson color of his carpet.

        Ah, but wait . . . Then there was a good part to the
            dream . . .

I was going to your house I had written a message
on luminous colored paper
softened by cubes of light pastel
and I was wanting to see you
and I gave the message to Marina Spheris
(Water of the World?)
and I doubted if it would ever be delivered
(Message in a bottle to the Water of the World?)
or seen by living eyes.

I think I saw you in the dream
from insurmountable distance
or I saw you as Stephen saw you
as I imagined he saw, when he told me what he'd seen— You
at the Human Rights Parade.
And how he told me
how he'd wondered—

> "Who is that guy. *Who is that.*
> I was sure, *he said, "it was some movie star*
> *or No —*
> *It was Brad!"*

Would you really marry Laura all over again?

Sleep baby. Sleep.

Arriving at the Civic Center, end of the parade
it *is* like looking for someone in a dream.
I see everyone else . . .
I see the queen in rouge and lace
lifting a polka dotted skirt for cheese cake . . .
I see the beautiful boy with lips laid back
one hand in sleep above his head . . .
I see two black men, rocking with the beat
one behind the ass of the other . . .
I see the dykes on bykes . . . the lesbian mother at the
        mike . . .
I pose . . . I see the men in ramrod leather . . .

But you do not see him, do you.

I see the gorgeous boy with olive eyes
who kisses the air in my direction . . .

I absorb therefore I participate . . .
I see two blond men in tie-dyed t-shirts
whirling and hugging each other . . .
I love to see men kissing in public I want to dance
to the music the women are playing . . .

But, you do not see him, do you.

No, I am going to leave now, and go eat pizza.
I am going to go into the restaurant bathroom
and watch the blood drop out with the plug
until the bowl fills up with bright red water
color of the child's carpet.

And then to remember its opposite:
Milking breasts, they were hot and hard
into the black smooth toilet bowl, *Blue Angel.*
White jet stream of mother's milk —
Explosion in the curved black water.

No matter how many yellow cars pass in the streets
you do not see him do you.

*Would you really want
to Marry Her?*

Will the colors of the pastel paper ever reach your hands?
No, because all of the sadness? All of it
sliding, under the table
touchable, touchable —
Slapped.
Heat from my hands, laced to yours
would lash like leather in the air of absence.

Let it go, let it go, let it go, let it.
Just let it.
My baby is dead.

*Well, from my experience, once both people
start having affairs, and agree on it
it's almost over, it's just a matter of time.*

It is all
just a matter of time, dear.
Death dear.
Paddling
in the midst of tumultuous time
keeping your head above water.
All a matter of flesh
and decay dear.
Feel the little rots in the porcelain?
Feel the slow age
under the facial skin?

> *Waiting.*

But my baby is not
dead today. See?
He's alive and outside eating cookies
in his red plastic sandals — *Oui Oui.*
I am waiting.
For the bougainvillea
to climb the walls of this study like living blood.
Waiting for it to wrap itself around the rafters.
My dripping, scarlet, fuchsia colored flowers —
Veins and vines
but will they grow inside here?

> David tells me they will.
> David tells me that with water and sun from the skylight
> and air from the open windows
> with fish emulsion (if the cat doesn't eat it
> if the puppy doesn't eat the cat)
> with care and patience they will
> devour my room with the memory of jungle drum Kenya.

> *The bird screams*
and I know that I love you.
At dusk, over the blue jungle of backyards
sounds are drawn out through a tunnel of caw food
and when the bougainvillea recalls the jungles of Kenya
then I will write you a great love letter
and I'll send it, even if I never see your living face.

> *The bird screams*
and I love him too.

In the jungles of Kenya
the blooms of the bougainvillea are so hungry
they pull down trees with their fierce loveliness
with their weight of crimson— Pulling
time down with the load.

Would I pull those down around me
for the beauty of the sound of the word?
No, my baby will not die, not yet, my friends
my memory
of your sweet face, even I
might live, even if it takes all the oxygen in this room
to pump out the smoke . . .   My words, my life
won't be a wasteful of paper.

      The bird screams
because love is not dying.
We have walked on the tangled waters
and both of us Gloria
seem to survive.
And the bougainvillea will help
remind me of blood.
And the bougainvillea will tell the No Bird
to eat it.

Trellis
(1978–1985)

On the Wallowy

for Gloria Frym

Earth tremor.   I felt an *earth tremor.*

(or was it just the house guests hunkering.

They love each other so
new & lovely
                    sitting on the sofa, his arm
and her arm — .
                    Great big smile an Immediate kiss.
Also a tenderness under the rib cage
                    bruising for that transitory
            ripest touch.

We come to imitation of initial urge
                                    wanting connection
to fill up the body with unmistakable This:

— SHOCKING WHITE SAMOYEDS ON AN YVES KLEIN BLUE —

Somewhere, sometimes, there's complete redness
azaleas in currant juice, huge satin lips.

                    "Don't ask," he said,
because he felt horrible. Most of those
on that particular couch did.

Creamy tears look thick in cup
    by candlelight.
                    Two stained hearts
sprout
            what seem to me
                            like milkdrops.

"It's really a shame," my father said driving, straight ahead,
"that people rarely love each other at the same time."
                                        (balanced.

                        Making a child is a similar thing:

She had always wanted to
gut-level wanted to
but he completely refused it
and it's already happened
now the questions begin.

            She's standing by the swimming pool
            confident, ready, but —
            There's no water in there!

                    I see.

            Yet she still dives
            yet she still swims through the air of the pool
            emptied, and arriving.

Don't ask me where maternal urge comes from.
I might say —
                From the tiny purple pony, thumb-sized
        I fed lettuce
                little nibbles of lettuce.

            (more an' more popcorn on the popcorn tree.

The lovely man so many women fall in love with
nods to the hostess who obviously adores him —

        "God," he says, "I wish she'd stop running around
looking like a servant."

            Makes ya feel kinda guilty don't it.

        But you know, Biewtifull, vut I'd Reeally like to see?
        It'z you in da serving position vunce in a vile, because

I'm getting prrity Tired of pooting out for a lot of
singal men an getting none of da same in Return. I don
care if you are a lonely, unnderfed bachelur, don't
arrive anymore uninvited at dinnur. I'm Tired of yer
lazy obserVations —
                    "Gee, I wish I had a wife."

   My good friend with hair like bees
her front room surrounded by foliage, many trees bloom
          & it's her birthday.
   "This makes me sad," she gazes out,
what's clearly passing.
                    "Every morning, I wake up
          and it's so beautiful
it really depresses the shit out of me."

   Rain stole the plum trees' radiance this year.
          Dry heat once made
each pulse bloom
                    comme clitoral attraction.

Listen, I tell this, fashion's not important —
"You're getting better," (meaning, more like Me) —
Emotional absence, a garbled intelligence
looks like a one-way
zipper Up.

               All I want to do is
               gather and accept it.
               Let us learn to walk a language —
               Incredible feat.

Ven he vants to stop me, he make a spraying motion vit
his fingas —
               I, am Spiderman.
               I got you in my web.

   Digital clock date
set to her birthday forever.

                              Spray paint on pony-tailed
                     part of his hair.
            Compulsive drawer
locked up in closet
                 keeps drawing anyway —

     Kick you with my cowboy boots na-na-na.

Nice to be reminded of innocent heart-felt feelings from sofa
but here on the wallowy, I don't see too many lucky ducks.

            Neighbor who I don't know well, comes
            to find her children. Two of them are
            here, another in her arms, but she
            couldn't (kept laughing) get a line out
            completely (slaps on thigh, ecstatically
            converted) "I saw these great, dark
            clouds, and then the writing— Sell
            Everything, I was hypnotized for years
            ran away with the baby, but my husband,
            excuse me, Am I talking too much? Maybe
            I shouldn't, but I always wondered, you
            know, when you walk the stroller—
            Some people have, you know, more light."

            Meanwhile, the kids (2, 3, & 4-ish)
            who I thought were heading for her house
            around the corner, have crossed two streets
            (one of them very busy) and have entered
            Safeway to steal a box of Crackerjacks.

He's his own girl friend, *blam / blam blam.*
Well, I guess, that's
one solution.
And a very short rope.
Looks to me, like contorted position —
Troll/mad/waiting/under/goat/clop/foot.

"Please don't eat me! I'm skin & bones!"
(little like a chicken wing
not much meat)

Type hunt/Type Hunt
can't escape it
what attracts us.
"She could solve everything,"
self-made Lie.
Type hunt/Type Hunt
only trouble is—
She was a very sad replica.

"Why a pop gun."
(with a cork on a string)

"What does a fucking Pop gun
for a birthday present mean.
I don't even *like* guns."

"I do," I said. (I mean
I enjoyed shooting it off
a couple times.)

Know what I saw?
Werner Erhardt, sitting on a dixie cup.
Thought it was a motorcycle. There was a straw. Couldn't go
too far. All the way to Georgia. Then I got scared. I want
to go home now. This made him *very* angry. So I had to run.
Nice ole rich man in Mercedes picked me up, saying he'd
transport me, friendly father-type, hearse black car, until
he slipped out and I saw around the corner that HE was in
butcher's clothes and *this* was a set-up I was already on the
line of tied-down women getting their throats slit and their
heads whopped off . . .

Hmmm,
I think I better tell you a gentler
bedtime story.

Ok . . .

> She was a chowist. She accompanied
> her doctor friend in Tibet to a distant
> monastery, and because he was an honored
> man, she was allowed to go with him.
> (This was quite rare.)
> But before the long journey through
> mountains in jeep caravan, he suggested
> something about selecting a stick,
> to keep the Blue Dogs back.
> (She wondered if *that* meant . . .)
> And then when they arrived, the holy gates
> were thrown open, and out rushed fifty,
> perfect, blue chows!

Well one of these mornings

You gonna rise up shinin'

Spread your wings

an' take to the sky

But until

that mornin'

There ain't a nothin'

gonna harm you

So hush

little baby

Don't

you cry . . .

They say
that at the hour
of the tremor
there's this sensation of waiting.

And beneath
that apprehension
you don't want to be touched.

Sometimes,

       somewhere

                   (heart so distant.

       Nothing trembles

but the memory of us.

The dog the cat the bird & the kid

for Catherine & Michael Freeling

Filled with odd notions this time of year . . .

So that's

what a sugarplum is,

Sweet Thought —

One day

I want to give him
my IUD for Christmas
and the next day
it's a canary.

It was just after visiting you Catherine
at Kaiser's Maternity Ward . . .

Michael and I

driving home lifted up
by second wind laughter.

Then I spot— *Your Basic Bird* store.
We have to go in there—

A chaos of clutter
Shrieks
one hand in a cage
and feathers unfocus . . .

"Personally
I thought it was a pretty flighty thing to do."

Do you think he'll at least like the *idea*
of a bird?

(His sister
almost threw up.

And when you couldn't join me for the latest 10 o'clock show
I went to *Turning Point* anyway out of sheer desperation.
What the men in the film basically had to say was—
     Do it, without any feeling.

Women at crisis point/regret either way.
One got the curtain calls and one
got pregnant.
     Shock hits your eyes, but
                         /that's not what I mean—
We all have to sometime succumb to our losses, envy
what's next, process our bitterness.

Locked in or locked up or locked out or
                              give way
wanting my bird to sing.

I feel the demands caving in from all sides I've constructed
and Catherine I'm afraid when you don't complain.

I must ignore my head cold
since the child has signs of pneumonia,
                              gurgles and squeaks,
          and his space man's lost
his helmet
          swallowed by a very red whale.

     "There's a dead guy in here," he whispers.

Then the plastic apple
               bongs & dings
water sound magnified
like the dream of the beak
big as scissors and I say—
                    "Bird Cage," in my sleep.

One does not complain about rain here
admittedly, but eyedrops 6 times a day for the dog
is a bit to remember.

Is it far
to across the street?

> *"But when, if Clovis dies*
> *a new boy'll come out of your stomach, right?*
> *And if a person dies, an Emergency*
> *truck'll pick 'em up and take 'em to the hospital*
> *Right Away!"*

I don't want a new boy. I want you to be careful.

"But the car Stopped. It really Did."

"You know what it's like to have an eyelash in your eye?
Well this dog's got fifty in each eye," said the vet.
Casually casual.
"We'll operate tonight."
And fear ran up on my tongue, blue tongue
because most dogs are dead when their tongues turn blue
harder to gauge anesthesia.
"Lots of vets won't even treat these chows. Like bears,"
he said,
"they give no expression of anger before they get you."

And the cat (wet cat) springs
onto my lap
just back
from the Humane Society
fixed.
              Try explaining *that* to a little male kid.

One thing about cats, they jump right back.
That's where the bird comes in.
                              Every cell
in the cat
        is poised
                and licking
                        and toying
                                with a single idea.

What if:
A man berates/a woman spanks/a kid kicks/a dog bites/a cat
        attacks/
a bird goes down by the cuttle bone
seed sprayed all over the carpet.
                                        Well,
            maybe it wasn't
                        such a good idea.

(Can someone have second regrets?

            I went to this pet supply store way out in
            Oakland, took Clovis with me and Torun,
            and this large thick man who owned the place
            walked with me up and down the platform,
            eyeing me also in the obvious way—
            "Come back after hours, six o'clock, I'll
            fix you up with a canary."

            Give a quick smile to the things that insult
            us, or Flip him the Bird, *what's healthy*.

Helping unload the cart at the CO-OP
Clove took the cardboard carton in one hand— Eleven
smacked on the floor.
                        (a spectacular slime
But the woman smiled
by the register.
She placed the twelfth egg back in my hand.

        "Some bird probably worked pretty hard on that."

Not as hard as we do though.

Catherine said it wasn't so bad for the second, though the
pain—
ka-Riest, one knows to expect, right into the heavy part
then it comes fast . . .
                        the worst

was her roommate
playing the TV straight for twelve hours
making her want to *really* scream.

Someone discovers there's a difference between
being "in love"
and continuing love for another.

                              Lafe, alone, is trying to
do-in Christmas.
                    Note on his locked door—
                    "No Hospital. My Way."

Clovis is coughing so hard he vomits and Nathan wants soup
made out of the baby. My sister is praying on marriage and
getting confused, while Gloria makes hand braided challah,
with the curving sweet taste of onions in it, and she slips
the loaf inside the unlocked door while we quietly upstairs
fuck. She's gotta get out of town now, to get out of all
history resentment, while we the perpetuators would like to
go AHHH and sink into some void whitened mindscape,
      without
our traditional/excessive/American/version of vision/called
over-give.

                  Nostalgia our only guide.

                  Memory the benefactor.

                  But— for The Child.

                  Which child.

Michael won't like the plastic shirts his mother sends to him
anyway.
          "All I wanted, was one good, solid,
white cotton shirt. That's all I wanted."

A good mother doesn't send you the size you wore in
        highschool.

96

She sends you cookies from your childhood
so that you can close your eyes
and go through with it.

But he was a prince last night, wasn't he?
Sitting up on his knees, lighting all of
the candles, eating alone at the large, round
table (tasting & silent) wiping his mouth
precisely, with his own napkin.

And when the doctor asked him, "Do you have any chest
        pains?"
he sat up straight and said, "Never."

And then the doctor went to the phone
came back smiling, said his wife had to call and tell him
about the neighbor's dog who's always dumping their trash
can.
Oh?
Yeah, but today, Rover came over and was littering as usual
but then Sheppy, their dog, was out joining him too
and when the doctor's kid looked out the window he said,
        "Hey, Rover asked Sheppy for luncheon."

And when I see Tango being led down the hallway of the
veterinary clinic, her hindlegs wobbling in a sideways direction
both eyes shaved and stitched, dyed green, the pink insides
of the lower lids drooping, I
can barely
look.

Do you think I should call the woman at *Your Basic Bird* store
tell her— This canary doesn't sing.
Or give it a chance to recover from Christmas.

        Give it something to sing for.

"But Laura," her voice travels 2000 miles,
"that's just one more thing to take care of,
that's just one more thing you'll have to *do*."

You know I spent one solid day
calling antique stores
looking for a fashionable old-fashioned bird cage
but all I got was a lot of information—

    (I consider it all useful
      by the way) . . .

              Arthur, the owner of one place
said that he had a Red Factor Canary, and that the story of
feeding them carotene to make them bright orange, simply
wasn't true . . .
          I didn't tell him that I liked the subtler
colorings of the brown-orange better, never have liked purity
in anything . . .
          But he got a mate for his bird, tossed in
prepackaged nesting materials, and then they had a whole
little bowl full'a—
          Yeah!   Itsy bitsy baby tangerines.

But they sing much better alone
the males do.
The females
only
      chirp.

Must we really make a whole lot of conclusions that stretch
        the limits of generality
and make another bad joke about that?

    chirp.

Catherine made Clovis a cape for Christmas.
Nathan called Clovis immediately, said—

"My Mama made *you* a cape for Christmas and this is a
    Secret!"
That didn't diminish its grand success.

Want a cup of coffee?
I'm so proud of myself that I know how you take yours.
It seems to say something
about the maturity of our friendship.

You know when I arrived at the hospital
with narcissus because they smell so good,
chocolate chip cookies and fresh Sumatra,
the latest copy of *Ms.,* which I grabbed
because it pictured Jimmy Carter, carrying
his belly at the 9 month load, plus a
homemade milkshake with lots of sherry
in it, and you said later, "I learned
something about you." All I knew was
that someone did a whole lot of that
kind of thing for me when I couldn't
move after labor, and her name was Helen,
and women I think keep passing it on,
as if love didn't have anything to do
with the singular gesture, but the
continuation of giving.

And maybe it had more to do with you.
That you were the one who went through
with it. You were the one who took your
IUD out, and then desperately didn't want
to be pregnant, and when you found out
you weren't, had it put back in again,
and then reconsidered, had it pulled the
next day, and in less than a week you
actually *were,* waiting till we were sitting
on the beach, eating heart-shaped ginger-
bread to tell me.

It's far easier to buy a canary. I'm waiting to hear one note.

Catherine, you complain less than almost any person I know.
How do you do it.
What's healthy.
I feel so damn bitchy lately.
Beginning to blame it on my safety coil for the possible
low-grade infection, plus those incredibly drawn-out
   (bleeding like a stuck pig)
                           "Want a tiny diaper?"
periods.

Tonight,
when a friend of his called and asked him to a party
and I could see how excited he was on the phone
all I could say when he hung it up
                        (and I refused
to even look at him)
            all I said was
   (turning the page)
                  "Too bad we don't like
                       the same people anymore."

Look,
every month there's a crisis point in our lives
though we know who we are, our priorities, what we can do—
Taking care of others is just one thing.

Maybe it's just as hard for a woman to relinquish
domestic control
as it is for a man to assume it.

And I can't help but notice
                  admire & grieve
when somebody else is
               splendidly in love

but a dog and a cat and a bird and a kid
and a whole lot of the other plus-plus-pluses
were all my choices
and now I'm going to stop blaming him.

Very soon I will make up my mind
whether to listen or not
to the voice I've been hearing— Laura, don't do it
without any feeling.

"Yeah, and a Tree can Explode!"

"You aren't writing much now,
you're in a dry season
        aren't you?"

                It's been raining so long
I didn't realize
                what exactly inside was so dry.

        Ok, let's submerge—
Big bubbles from the tub.
                With a slosh
        and a Ding

    "I brought it back to life"

vrrooom VRROOOM

                ((buckles & chains))

        Sing for yourself, Canary.

Memory, the Meat Flower

for Philip Pahner

Try hard *not* to imagine an elephant, not to imagine an elephant not to imagine an elephant.
All I see is an Elephant.
Taking mental revenge.
Over the edge down the slide he said— Took me, he Dragged me to the end of this pier, at the mouth of the ocean, No, I couldn't swim, and he turned on the faucet that wet down the slide, so it was slippery, he had to *grab* off my hands, detach them like this. He pushed me and half way, at the bump I let go. I died. I was sinking. I drowned and everything got greyer gradations of grey. I had to be resuscitated, and my parents, what's incredible, watched all of this, calmly, at the foot of the pier. Those two, back there.
Now chalk swirls connect him to the smoothest of circles. Pink folds to yellow, a rounded aquamarine. He pictures a chamber that gets the double beat bump back, going in with his hands, around and around.
The surgeon felt the breast like a surgeon feels a breast. She thought about chicken parts. Don't buy chicken parts, because they hack off the cancerous section, sell you the legs. He repeated the "joke" about body of a woman, stuffed down meat grinder, coming out ground beef. Don't buy ground beef.
I had a long cloth doll with elastic bands that attached to my feet. So we could dance of course silly. You can buy a life-size rubber woman to go to sleep with now. (You can give a girl an enema.) You can put her in a chair, say Good Morning Irene. You can have your own little rubber companion. Why do you keep repeating these things, do you keep repeating these things.
You ever been to Montana? Ever been to *Foul Mouth Jean's*? This one night, you should have seen her, when these five fifteen year old girls, who didn't know what they'd walked into, walked in. There was a perfect lull, I mean the pool balls

stopped clicking and there even was a pause in the TV commercial, and old Jean rose up and hollered out CUNT.

Kids in Alaska
put seal oil on their Cheerios.

That makes me sick, that's creepy,
that's disgusting says the girl, looking at the picture of magnified
intestines like many sausage white fingers softly intertwined.

I told
him I believed that a body leaves the body, that there is a top view,
an ecstatic, amniotic, kind of acceptance, released from it— Light—

We held hands around the table, and the youngest one whispered,
Thank you Jesus, thank you, for all this good stuff. And everybody giggled,
but everybody said "Again," every evening, and the kids especially wanted to do it again, do it again . . .

Dying is the hard part,
the impossible birth part, but what we're trying to find out, is why
Death itself, leaves them, so often, with this beatific expression.

He accused himself for living. He couldn't get to sleep. Couldn't
do without the candle.

Now I lay my soul to take.

Goodbye black
calla, meat flower, old sickening aroma.

It was at the bump, on
the slide, and this tunnel getting darker.

No more oxygen mommy. At that moment, letting go.

Goodnight octagonal.

Goodnight
round.

They say the light there at the end, has the greatest
sense of humor.

Star jasmine

will be one day

what we on entering

smell.

Gate's Waiting

Nothing seems to matter so much as being *right there,*
engaged in the way of wording it. All the rest is circular excuse.
And like most lives, go on living. But unlike most, there's that men-
tal worm, a need for this underearth groping. How to inch it out,
how pass the dirt of existence, bubbles in the mud the unexpected
percolation, what we used to just *do,* not call or say, stirring in
the stick, down deep in the bucket so as not to get stuck for a mo-
ment.

Association is the molecular link and we trust it. Just found
the lost box of Red Indian Clay not used since the three of us
plastered our faces, stood suspended in the kitchen as it tightened.
The cracks laughter made on our mud masks. Washing it off we
felt wind burned. That was right before your van left town.

And

left us.

We discover new ways to circulate around absence, roller
skating down Shattuck where the cement's wide, doing figure 8's
on my red Kryptonics—

(She'll have to learn how to control herself.

You can unhook the phone though someone may need you. At the
moment you may need yourself. But the standard black phone
disembodied from connection, might as well be a poodle made of
china, by the window and the African violets, near a scatter of mail
in the sun.

"Thanks for another quiet evening!" she yelled down
the drive, and her laugh had the quality of swallowing several round
goldfish.

You are happiest when everyone in the world leaves you
and your friend alone, so that you can put one tiny box inside a
small box, inside a bigger box inside.

Remember when the three
of us were careening down the sidewalk, all arms linked, half-pint
of milk in my hands? We were flashing in stride all out of our minds
glad to be right in the middle of that day.

There can be jealousy
between us, though different with women friends, not as excusable?

Most who get shots of silicone for the enlargement of their breasts are doing it for the approval of other women.

In the middle of Broadway, he rolled down the window, "Hey look-it, her chee-chees are blinking!"

Uncomfortable, we regard the hard-packed image of voluptuousness, and assume it's only *their* obsession.

On a previous occasion the same magazine, aroused in me a very strong longing to fuck, as the old Dodge Dart passed the Seven Sacred Pools and ended up in an empty parking lot. Despite the steering wheel, a sleeping child in the backseat, the power of exhibitionism got me wanting to want.

You might find that philosophically repugnant, but she had uncoiled on the rock, where everything was ripe, was spume and spray, dangling like banana flowers. The young boys were hammering on wood behind the orchids. Whales let go leaping and everyone could float in the waves of a buoyant Pacific. He put the flashlight, lit, down the crotch of his pants, while the fires along the cove looked primitive.

Nikki-Nikki Tembo, Oh So Rembo, Oo Ma Mouchie, Gamma Gamma Gouchie.

Never-never satisfied are you. With what has been caught between the covers of a book. Maybe it's not so much unlike my father who I called long-distance and who had to cut it short, because he was in the middle of a meeting, meaning money, meaning, never-never satisfied are you.

Money appealed to them, money in a jar. A tin lid with hammered in coin slot. The shake of the coinage and the weight of it increased, money-money smell on their fingers. Coin spread out over the carpet.

Trying to read, I can't help but feel it's pitiful, telling my only child he should play tic-tac-toe by himself now.

I'll meet you by the bubbler in the lobby. I got Milk Duds down my mitten in my pocket. I wish we were still girl friends, sitting in the dark, waiting for the great big image.

You put a robin in a shoe box. You put a stone on the earth. This is the animal graveyard. You can not step within the circle where the animals are without causing yourself grave danger.

While drivers abandon their buses in

the blizzard, and your child has you wild with cabin fever, we hedonize the day above the tennis carpet green watching the female champions.

But what I liked best was her temperament, how she'd nod her head *Yes* to the shots which were perfect when she missed them.

I can't knit, can't crochet, don't have the proper mental attitude, and get antsy when my fingers won't function.

If this is elitist, it is also non-profit, as were the Christmas ducks. It took all of his strength to strangle them. It took all of my nerve to pick one up. Sticky stuff of duck down, hot from the dunking tub, warm limp body of bird in my hands, the intimacy of entrails, and like many a modern wedding, just a minute to consume it— Few words, small bird, timing is a shock.

The worst might be rutted in avoidance, or stuck on repetition which is the dishes not art, which is the irritation of the needle saying, tation of the needle saying, tation of the needle saying—

And they lived happily, ever, after. Or until Love do us part.

We are parted but it hasn't departed. You departed but we aren't disengaged.

Movement is a form of mystery to me. But then so is Roger the Lodger, who decides to remove our blue armchairs, and places them outside by the trashcans. (Oops, wrong planet.) He puts the metaphors into the ground so to speak—

"I have transplanted the small wild rose bush, which symbolizes Clovis, away from the choking environment of the two big lemon trees."

Right-O-Rog! Don't forget on the corners you must put on your hiccups. I goggle at your departure from the norm. Not unlike the dog-bear, racing with my underwear, ready for a romp on the hearth rug.

What we need is a stone fireplace like the one you describe, in the woods, under snow, in isolation. Or maybe what we need is a typewriter like a fireplace, one small corner that is warm when you come to it, a place where everything can fuel.

Here in California, Ah Sweet California, which may resurrect the quality of the living joke, I saw in mid-January,

106

a quince tree in bloom, as I skated past the future—

(as she skated

past the future—

"Mom, hurry up, the gate's waiting for you!"

Trellis

for Willa & Ayler

A small blond girl brings a dark haired woman, a beautiful woman who is sitting in the grass, legs together to the side very feminine, a small girl in a short plaid dress, brings her mother these flowers, a handful, for she is in love with this woman, strange beautiful woman, and the woman seems amazed by the child, wonder and amusement, as she sits so carefully seductive in the grass, with her dense red lipstick and polish, the woman has waves in her hair. I wonder if the woman will accept them, the flowers. The child is so tentative, careful with her love. But of course she accepts them, her laughter accepts them, and everybody is glad.

But how now to reconcile the oldest hostility, breast against breast, flower crushed, tooth nail and hair. How to skin those feelings, let them swell to a drum, coming back with my belly to deliver them.

No, no, the gift's never good enough. Child not the daughter she's supposed to be. Very much "supposed to be." Wanting each other silenced. Brutal reconciliation. None in the freezer chest, none.

I needed a saddle, not a bullet jacket. I needed a saddle to escape. I asked the groom for one, preferably soft and wide. He left the stable and returned. With a Band-Aid. "Here's a good saddle for your horse."

Insults & injury blew the surface acceptance of everything she'd secured as refuge around her woman friend. Wanting it easy not difficult— Now, we need the gritty feel of cleanser to rub'n rub up against, not the endless o.k. (denial) of just *letting it go*.

After the hot steam espresso of anger came calm, a sisterly benediction. Long stretch of water galactic with light— The steps up were smooth and uncluttered. We climbed to her home where her mother would give us milk butter and bread, meaning affection, her motherly love.

★

I wrote her— I've lost the old passion. How can I make it *move* anymore, push it waterlike Over without the old passion. Is it just being pregnant, this slow river I'm on, sittin' in a fishin' hole of contentment?

But she wasn't content, because she wanted that passion more than anything, in her, more than coffee and cigarettes, she wanted that fiire, to float on her water, needed oil and a flame, needed juice, his quick juice for her brain to push over. But no, she'd be pushing a baby. That's different, not sexy. Old elephant pants. And yet blood engorged volume excitement *come on* — Huge mammals hump up in the ocean.

Or consider the weightless sex of the net veined dragonflies, who settle in tandem on my knee. She rests the tip of her long curled tail on the base of his neck, he bends his tail under— It sticks to the base of her abdomen. Holding that position, immobile, as if forever, making a blue heart shape.

He rubs his hardness up behind her largeness for fun— He can grope her symmetrically then. He splits apart his pants— She does and doesn't want to see— He twists a mammoth worm in mud around his finger. She goes down, going down, to engorge upon connection, for this is her biggest turn on.

Nudge, said the mother. *We Nudge,* said the one. So they nudged all day in the Valley of the Sun.

Delighted to find out that the guy she'd had the crush on was a total boor, for his baseness aroused her, he was no longer a threat. "You can have me," she said, so sober it scared him. He belonged in her satchel full of kicks to call up. I'm a Man, he mused, staggering. Not a Thought.

Her husband now is totally engaged, talking with another man. Both discredit by ignoring her presence. But she has two dolls, which she undresses in front of them. HaHA she says to herself. They pay no attention. The dolls have abnormally long penises for dolls. She moves the hand of each doll onto the sex of the other, amusing only herself.

All right, she'll go off to ride her own horses. She doesn't need their saddle. She doesn't need a rein. She doesn't need any of their intellectual get-up. The creature can sense the other creature inside her, and moving between her legs, the animal responds.

Fly, said the mother. *We Fly,* said the

two. So they both flew together to the Valley of the Moon.

Someday her real man will return to her, and not with his needs, his hunger or his burdens. He'll come lightly back into her original courtyard, and his skin will be cool and water fresh. Then nothing will interfere with their darkness, almost familiar, nothing will hinder their conceptional kiss.

In the garden every light was cuddling up the animals— Small pockets of haze around the rabbit babies and phlox. In the stable *hallelujah* all together we were moving, in a vibrant local hum, in the sun a kind of purr was in the air was on the oats, and as the trellis rose above us, a warm wind fell.

★

I slept on your name, Eden, place of my pleasure— A confirming light glowed with belltones collecting in answer to my question, which way will the ring swing, back & forth or around.

She came out two months early to show me her vulva. It was important that I see this fruit-like part of myself, though what entranced me most was her serenity, for this was a calm and knowing child.

Feeling strong— Stand, positioned on pier, facing smooth water. Feet parallel, shoulders down, head up higher. Full-bellied woman turns, sinks to her holding stance, arms straight up, in control of each motion. The people jabbering on martini boat ride by in silence. She releases a soft O sound.

Looking up, we see cumulus piles, skyward climbing. "The power inside more than 50 atomic bombs," he said. The pilots dip with respect and run their little props home, but thundering rain is my headdress.

Knees, a sweet portrait of knees, fine and girlish, by the sand, in a daze, before the stone wall. You know how fast she can run, how still she can stand, quietly, ready, how rarely she has gotten down on them.

He wants to paint the house black. Yes, including the trim. She wants to paint it fleshly, say a warm melon color, cantelope and cream. He wants a sophisticated archive. She wants a borning room. How can they agree on any name.

By holding up the same umbrella?

110

Everything was drenched with a palette of greens drenched early morning semiconscious aromatic field, that moves to throw its moisture into bursting. Forth and forward, swishing on through, to the middle where she'll want to lie down, and be held. Not necessarily kissed. Just held, all around, held in, on his shoulder, squeezed, encircled, his breath on her brow.

She will come sliding into town out of one amazed mother. Only after the fall did labor turn hard. Dream myself back into that garden, before the bite, vicious, snakey twist of it tightening, round my abdomen. I will give in, float under the wave, and bring her forth with the pushing swell of it. Mutual waterdrift into this world, with her name flying first to guide her, There— place where she might find her own pleasure. *Jouissance,* they will say, *jouissance, jouissance,* a rustling reminder of reeds around the harbor, as her bow bulges in, a widening chorus of bells— Dove skin Chime lamb button baby, prisms of glass shivering with color, giving in now into her unfolding rose, deliver us whole. Bathe us and bring us up together again, as we were, in the swing, above the garden.

In a Motion

The dangers of drifting while driving, in a daze— Loosening the reins that last ride on Eagle. I had the premonitions that day, galloping alongside Old Farm Road, newly spread gravel hid the edge of asphalt, my horse nicked— Sliding, weight of horse flesh— Thrown, into a splash of view, as if I *were* the landscape, skid-hot palms, even liking that later, the wakeful, unexpected, stinging *smasheroo*. It all felt familiar, as if I'd read that page (somewhere), or someday, like "The End," plucked out of the saddle, oddly marvelous and shocking, like birth, but not squeezed, rather— Freed from the tiddly winks of shape.

To summon inside— The brave shining warrior, glittering hero of the skies with flaming sword, astride a horse so white, you *know* you are ready, to meet and overpower The Dreadful. I've got my firm together now, my word drawn up, to hold and to swing into warning. Big "L's" begin lifting, for lightness and levity, raising the sediments Up in the body. *L* is for *Lucia*, I said with my slipper, for all of the liquid that rises forever and falls into falls, to further the flowing, to keep us in motion.

Now each yellow girl on the bright red background of my new knit vest, reaches up to catch a heart above her head, while the boys down below around the border are running and flexing— They all warm my chest. They are not your modern children, who expect to be questioned, throwing up the hooves to their little lamb costumes. To resist what this culture insists on, strikes a light that cuts fad image into doubles, until a million brooms sweep wild water in a panic, and yet, this is such a tiny world with a placemat of maniacs, so why not try to set it right.

How to walk the white steed, each step lifting, and carrying, and placing to stand. The electrical smell falls in a ring at your ankles. You *are* the shining rain. You draw a Number 1, in a motion, to the sun— The globe itself hovers there before you. Yes, you can touch it, give it a little "L—" That's what it's come back for, to set you on your way, gladly, with a hum— An approval.

Iscador

Mistletoe kiss me sting— a waspish. To embrace the poisoned leaf,
white berry bloodless. Poke that fire started somehow on sheer ice.
What melt can do, what flame say. Snow, well . . . even covers.
Into the long white dwelling cave we dug our blue. Little bears
with noses (sniff) so round our inner heat shone through. Yet don't
forget those freezing tips— Even cool bath water burns it.

Hearth can't wait another year. Need ignition symbol roaring, right
here. Else in cool we work a bend, to pillar of the past, look back,
to stone. So much gather, sticks fall. Leaves let go. My room
separates from the house, a crack of sky. Now is time to knock
things back, air tight. Copper plate-back firelight for Mood Woman.
Call me (wall me) what you will. *Shhh,* he touches, *nuff now.* Precious
heat against such cave. Conch-song-echo, wing, waves, roll back
to suck the living. Someone younger comes to wonder, watch and
poke and feed the fire.

Saw and snap of small glass ampule, pushing in the luckless sting.
Makes a ring of red in you, a swollen nest, a nauseous knot. You
cannot clearly— "Come, Wake up." Days remaindered for a dime.
Better sue the cream off that. Now is time to knock things back.
See thick nails quick up our lean. Tight and squeezed like fancy
knees. By Summit Pass. The height and squeal of car appeal. We
drove into another climb— Circling up round shiver lake. It made
us safe inside, in close, where wool and wheel and cloth slipped.
Fires blazed along the road. A's framed the freeze to come, but
yellow and red roar now instead. Hot and cold here meet their net,
their duel, their test. From root to skull, from flower to flow.
Harden, soften, freeze or flame. They set a fire in my name.

Returning to the World

"Sleep is the Mother of God."
— *Flannery O'Connor*

When I heard that thunder, I rose up like a happy animal. The
window was wide, it was a hard straight rain. I leaned towards
that freshness, beyond the family photos, having just unlocked the
last room to my heredity. And what did I find there— In the ruins?
(The contents glistened like candy-preserved antique toys.) Greed,
for material possession, which must be the top layer over some other
layer of need. But there in the icing of the dreamwork, I spied the
perfect arthritic bicycle, made entirely of wood, every curve, each
spoke— I knew it would collapse if I touched it.

My father did give me permission to ransack the past. Might I even
say he encouraged me? But it was *my* move flicked the cellular
switch, self-repulsion on the structural level, collapsing the castle,
setting the bones on fire, exhausted under the noiseless hum. I
tightened up the reins on life itself, until my hands ached as if from
a horse ride. But we know the fingers were just too eager to take,
that conscience doesn't want you to cheat one bit, that life *is* cons-
tant in its demand for you to give, and that you cannot control
The World.

From the first sign of hardening, to my birthday, nine months.
Now I understand the significance of cake. The unfrosted one-layer
with light. How I want it to glow in the waiting-room— Healed.
The unseen moves upward as the physical turns stone. *"Rise up
from out your carved condition."*

Each day it grew harder to move. Positioned with pillows, I would
lie in the afternoon with my eyes closed, and the sun would flood
in between worlds, redwood beams grasping the whiteness.
Everything so still, it was a blessing that stillness. The plum tree
full of flower, a gentle feeling as sleep came gratefully wrapped in
soft swaddling.

Not who to blame, not even who do I forgive, just this need to be completely held. To give oneself over, to skin the shining seed— Then to bury it. It was a long, slow rain, and it was coming from me, pulled from me, aching, until even the smallest birds bathed in it, and new life came up on its own grief. I will have slept from the Birth of Light to the Death of Darkness, and then my time is come to term, this spring. Still, I have these hours, returning to the world, while the rainwater pours, streaming over the roof of this room, and I am deep in my comforter.

Go Round

The longest day will drive a crack, till *Jubilate* windows in. Three parts that braid begin to fly— That something singing, overlapping. White roses on the fire lit. The stick once put begins to curl. A wheel is rolling sparks for ten. She feels it here, but *far away*. High golden hills remind the day of Saint-John's-wort. One yellow cup upon each end. Asha found three little bowls. The tones are gliding through the light. Mountains can appear we wave— And roll in dusk and dark till then. Because the small ones cannot stop. We find a way to circle so. We close into a fire pop. Open also leaves have room. And grow with pushes following through. We sing to leap the last of it. The nuts are gathered in a cup. The arc is scent, the curve a boat. To row and row the blinding stream. We hope to cast a shadow yet. A firm trail makes me follow up. We turn and run descend upon. To beat a beat upon the rim. A kiss in light before a name. The same few rise. Until she flew. The angel woke to be a bird. And never once the same again. The turquoise chamber turning parts. Lemon mint upon the flame. Old treasure sack. The tones do chime. And nut hats six can climb sky high. We wave we wheel around the bend. Though amber changed the wending way. Sinking deep in Lion's mane. Go round she say to sign your flame. Seven stars are shining bright. The round is fine— Just out of sight. We see it dry to golden sheets. Though wet was once all flick and stain. Today will not remain again. Go round she say— Go round to me. And let the lifting bird come through. The gate is raised, the sun can too. Go round— Go round. Today is different, yet the same. A new— A new. Goodbye in waves for sinking down. Often time to *see* and *bend*. Around she say. Once more again. So ashes breathe— Around me now.

Inner Everest
(1985–1986)

From: Free Rein

Something is met here, a strength of will, in a silent quarry, notch of stone. Almost an absence of air can you hear it? Up to the peak of the flip-deck fantasy. A window flies open and something shoots through. She didn't know *what* she was riding to this, but now can't get the arrows out. And her little disappointments are flattering to him. Fluttering, all, the way he'd look, in navy, nice, a suggestion of bicep. Lying way back on the saddle, Sky, he catches her hand, she tightens the pommel. Certain a notion of safety, that nothing will happen— It's all in her head, until they spot, What? That horse on the loose.

★

She wasn't a girl like other girls were. Something in her reared and flew. One with the rein and one with the muscle, held the hair the impossible hurdle. Back, far back, in our dark soul the white horse prances, lurking in ancestral genes, Sephardic, in the deep Prime Woods, where her neck snapped, and blood woke, but she rode again to learn it all— *Uphill fast, downhill slow.* The softest rattle from across the field, one golden pail could perk up a ripple for more, More. You may feed your fear in the form of an apple, your lust in the form of a pear. You may place your saddle like a layer of cake upon another. Be gentle with the touch on your reins. Laughing, her friends, rode the backs of the brood mares, half-eyed and honied with the summer heat, through the split melon smell of the mown fields. And happy was her name.

And now has come the season of stain. She feels it blaze towards some last chance and tries to catch the meaning fast. The glorious bursts out— Tree shaped, in dazzling dress, while the small hill on which she stands seems to nearly crumble. Look, there is such mercy above color and grateful water, a body that can *move*, towards an honesty that has to ask for the ability again, to hear it right— What shines? Behind those leaves that fire and blind us, caught as we are, too far, too close— Ah, Great Love can open us. Let us see our lives for what they are, yet nurture a call for kindness, ask that the words come simple and plain, as food after fasting. Delicious to drink in the miracle, light. Benign, a warmth to wrap her in, before it is time to wake.

★

The angel of the equestrians is with us again this morning, shining through benevolent weather. She has slipped into the quince for a change of dress, that ugly duckling of the apple family. When the horses get a whiff of that pungent sweetness, little wings in their mouths start pulsing and we glide. You may not believe in this angel of the equestrians, but she moves with us under the tall trees, she leads us through the darkness toward the track. She is beautiful, just beautiful, if only we could hear her laugh, at the mention of— "A death wish to ride with us." She knows there is no escape. That the quince will return, even if they're taken, even if you have to wait a year. She sits between the blue reins of the least best bet, leaving all the losers in the dust.

"Make winter nice, and bright, just invite me, by repeating my name." Repeat without thinking. A sleigh over snow before any cars come, the incredible quiet, loaded with soft layers, blankets and horse bells, her happy face, encircled— His hands, the *shush* of the runners, oblivious horse flanks, some tender hesitation till he speaks the truth in deep smooth Italian. Sweet, sweet cold, makes hot the head. "How old are we?" His hands make her shudder in the carved loveseat, which tips, knocked over, like a cord of wood— His yanking the banner to her foolishness. Waking up to the matches in the hidden niche— "You asked for it," while the one she imagines (he will always stand alone), tips sherry by the mantel in his big black boots.

★

The profound blankness of a deep trance, the crystal's coma would now be nice, as the needle, drill, and scalpel scrape— She pictures the power— Unleashed, through her own gloved hands, the stallion allowed to work and *breathe,* up on the top in large green circles, fields alone, the wind released— Just to imagine that acceleration, the subtle pressure, leather, response, and liking that, just right between, while the others walked and knew not. She rode— Flew, over pain all bruised and roses swollen, to loosen the bands that clench the teeth, calming down with talk and pat, to await the golden awaited day, when the face is freed like the moon floats, over the fields and rounds of hay, the memory filled with the smell of leaves pressed dark with fruit and corn fermenting, trees raked, and the air reborn, *renata* to you, who never was even half afraid by the boot caught trapped in the steel stirrup, the power of all unspoken words, while sighting that trail of glittering sequence, that leads, when followed, to dangerous knowledge.

Meteor showers purge the Indian summer sky, while boys lie down, sulfur spent, in the middle of midnight cornfields, shorn, to watch for sudden stars. To see some birthday being born. Their mother now remembers well that perfect face of infancy, falling into her fallen arms, pleading with her to re-turn. She hums, she waits for the proper blow to strike her rocking chair with sense. What knocks. She isn't a mother like other ones are. But sings as she canters through the wood, baroque tunes that feel of meadow and fox hedges, French horns. No leaves left. And life too dear. Babe in the arms of memory, sears like a shooting star. She should have a blaze on her forehead, to erase her bent— The provocative rip. A modest impulse, high noon. November plainly provides, visibility (naked, stript, cold). The heavens too will open and speak in the language of lasting iron and rose.

★

Great bunches of gigantic gardenia breed and bloom like creatures. She must go to them, their expanding fragrance, for they are at the height of their fullness— Voluptuaries of skin. She is drawn to them, shining in the dark, and gathers an armload to her, as if she could press them into her. She would have them transformed into some living gown, and then be born most feminine. But as the flowers fill her hands, she sees that the blooms are melting, and she knows that she has to act now, for the petals are falling, scattered. She would make a deep white bed of them, she would silence the crushing of the hooves. If only this were possible, she would fill his arms completely, as the flowers are filling hers.

The one that she feared all along, horse without rider, that lucky stud, who stalked through the woods and lit up her doorstep, who called but hung up in the middle of the night, his nose is now milky, his muzzle's in her hands, there is nothing to speak of as bliss descends. Here where the trail stops, she steps out of stirrup and walks into air, this wonder of dream flesh, this ponderous wing. With the stroke of his hoof the fountain is burbling, raising her high above carnal injunction, and she knows it's the ultimate ride, the end. For a moment, afraid, they'll worry about her, but— How can she part with this superlative, mounting and climbing the staircase to heaven— She never had a laugh so long and good.

★

Hush, was whispered, *guard it.*) There is nothing to be done now, listen. Nothing you can do. First snow descends most silent. Falling through worlds to be our covering, our rest, putting us back beside the woodstove, where the copper pot sings for its supper, and the mouths of the children breathe against the frozen glass. There is nothing to accomplish, no test. Just allow that flower, to break its sheath of ice, and warming, bloom in brightness. No one has to take it. Nothing to be said. Let it open toward the hills, the higher hills. Let it be the song on which you rise, even as the snow descends, and absence animates the landscape, even at this time of darkness, *sing.* For tomorrow will amaze us, as the constellation rides, and moonlight doubles (in the heart of the beholder— Balancing the curving slopes of white.

In Regard to Him

Here is a man who can drive women crazy. He enjoys the different flavors of their sex, but is burdened by the female gender. As soon as he feels himself falling in love, he pulls back, as if shocked into memory. He knows he could make himself miserable, by choosing too constant a picture, yet has a hard time peeling the fruit of his heart. Hers is a plum he has handled. A man of cerebral quality, not brilliant enough to convince her with lies, he attends to his physical person. He should take long hot baths, doused with lavender, to increase the skill of his patience. He is a social being, yet part of him would lead a very private life— (a small stone cottage in some remote province)— to live there and fuck the woman he loves and to eat great food from her plate. This woman exists. His perfect match. But he refuses to turn to the bookmark, preferring to study the rational list of items that fit the bill. She has one or two words for this bill. It might be better if she were to reside across country, for he likes an object out of reach, to pursue, while she lives in the open, a curious mix, vibrating at a special frequency. He always takes note of good vintage, but she wants to drink the warmed wine of his mouth, eat the courses of his perfect body. This is the way her mind works, but only in regard to him. He is pleased, but she shouldn't be so obvious. He is drawn to her forthright spunk, then repelled. She understands him better than anyone, though she hardly knows him after all. She is generous and selfish, so is he. Together, they appear, a striking couple of opposites, for her lust line follows the water pipe. He reveals to her the way. She worships him out in nature. He respects her opinion because she is accurate. He would like everything to be of the very best quality, and this comes naturally to her. Initially, he wants a woman harder to get, but once gotten, he gets the difference, between action and actuality. He can lose interest fast, but tries to convince himself, while she always renders surprises— Keeps him on his toes, up over the barn sink. She is capable of serving and creating much happiness, but he mistrusts this little word, "happy." His European perspective finds her naïveté startling. He is fiercely independent. She is lively when alone. He's a dedicated father and son, but resents the necessary indulgence. Many women fawn over him. But nobody knows what he's up to. She smiles. She loves to touch his cheek where she's just left her lipmark. This is one of the ecstasies. She hopes it will only continue to matter. He likes to be shocked. By cold water and laughter. Because he is fluent in so many languages, they say that he is great in bed. So does she. But he flaunts one lover in front of another, and doesn't realize this is a sign of misogyny. He won't put up with a bunch of crap, won't have it on the place. She laughs. For he wants things flexible, his way. He can respond to the instant, but plans months in advance, confident, yet vulnerable underneath. She becomes premenstrual when she feels him withdraw. She gives him something beautiful or useful, though he confuses her birthday with another's. He likes to be elated, accomplished in risk, while avoiding emotional turmoil. He wants a complicated pattern to fall into place. She wants to be the recipient of his masculine will, but can tell he's arranging another life, pre-nuptial promises, like pearls dropped in ink, while she's writing her own dismay. He's like one person inside another inside another inside another, and this fascinates the child in her. He keeps trying to fulfill perfect pleasure, but at the moment of fulfillment, all pleasure is lost. He retains apparent grandeur, even when "spent," she says, "wasted." She loves to almost make him pass out. He could loosen his limits. She wants the boundary of his arms. He might learn to be a kinder person, but he'd rather not answer that question. She won't believe that he's ever getting older, for she could behold him forever. This thought makes her very sad. He too has his feelings, fleet moments of gladness, but his plans can't always include her, and her notions are like those of an impressionable. She would bathe him in springs, rub his feet with healing oils, restore him with yielding sleep. She would ennoble his room with flowers, for she wants to undress him, button by button. She wants to drop onto her knees. To devour his lobster. To hear him say again — "You're the closest I've come yet." She has lived long enough with hostility. Neither of them wants to repeat old mistakes. Money seems to purr in his trousers. She spends very little but has a lavish mood. He goes for the limit. She digs dirt in the garden. He likes painted nails on glamorous women, but soon their coy egos annoy him. She would come to him quickly if he were fallen or sick, for he has opened her flower, and now it fills her whole person. She's more beautiful when she is around him. Both women and men are drawn to her, for she is like some living statue in their midst, singing to make your heart break. But now a liquid whiteness fills the vision of her days, as she sees him moving away from her, heading for another's island. And yet what is terrible, can also be redeemed. Perhaps if she holds still long enough. If he tastes her meal made of music. Then the arrow of her love song will strike its bird, only to bring forth new life.

The Feast

She would place herself at his table
not immediately beside him but
close enough, so that they could catch the crystalline
moment when eyes click,
for he would be her banquet incarnate
her heart's complete meal,
the feast of all flowers, magnanimous.
Each blue star gone singing —
Each lily petal pool —
O it might be less risky
to move further away
but this nearness is part
of the surging
of summer, is the silver ink of his name.
She would leave a glistening trail
down the length of his body
imagined in moonlight, all bare
and erect, amidst the tall drenched grasses of the pasture.
She would hang a tiny bunch
of green grapes from each earlobe,
lift her hair to prepare him
for the curve of her neck,
wearing only satin
beneath everything, in secret,
in sure anticipation of his smooth descent,
and she would be breathing
away the time it takes
before the first of their perfect courses.

Partners

He had spoken of this ride for a while now, how he wanted to find a hidden trail, take a lunch in the saddlebag, spread a blanket on the leaves, drink wine, eat cheese and make love. They would ride long and hard. They'd feel the sitbones in their asses, the chaffing of contact— All this rubbing aroused her— He called it his kind of foreplay, and she had eyes for no man but him. Yes, she would follow him into the forbidden, on any unmarked trail. He thought someone should meet them with the basket, but she thought she could carry it all in her knapsack. This was how they lost one of the halters. This was how their picnic seeped and crumbled in the bag.

It was a greyish, November day, and the last of the colors were mature, wine-stained, noble colors that suited the darkness of his face, as he pointed out the golden grove of larch trees in the distance, and she admired the bleached blond stalks of standing corn, and even the grey of the hardwoods stripped down, the papery rust of the carpet, appealed to her in his mood.

She was glad, after miles, holding onto the knapsack, to finally find a place to get off. The horses were hot, also eager to rest, and she tied them to trees, while he uncorked the white wine, and they shared it right out of the bottle. The marinated salmon was as sweet and delectable as his own tongue, and she didn't know which she would rather, but ravenous, and he fed her bits of the pink, fleshy meat, and she spread shallot cream cheese on a bagel. They ate until they felt rested, amused with each other. He listed the caretakers of his past, scooped a handful of moistened meringue crumbs from the bottom of the bag, forced big bites of apple in her mouth. She suggested the core go to the horses, feeling warm in the leather of his jacket, dazed from the ride and the good white wine, and all that she craved now was him.

He lay back down to rest upon the crushed leaves, and she slipped comfortably on top of him, kissed him with her mouth, kissed him with her teeth and her marinated tongue. She loved looking at his face like this, laid back. She called it beatific, his manly smile, the

128

texture of his skin in need of shaving, those sleepy lips of his, flirtatious eyes— But he had this ever-conscious time sense.

It was too late now, he thought, to lose themselves. In the leaves like this. If they didn't go now, they'd be riding in the cold wet dark by dinner. She could wait. For she had, she had. And it was probably this difference in temperament, which would help them to survive. She had a kind of faith in survival, and believed in the luck of their being together. She didn't want to say the wrong words or act wounded. She just wanted to ride by his side. There would be time, some other time. He pulled her up to him then, took her in the circle of his plaid woolen arms, and she felt like the nucleus of his world, being held. They mounted, and headed back over the pike, onto Shun Toll Road, where a chill was descending with the night as its costume, but the glowing tips of their smokes both lit up, as they breathed, and moved the horses, down the darkening road.

Eating Alone

Sitting here by the firelight with the blanket up— Your big glass
frames, I adore, looking over at you, when you lift your eyebrows
quick and add, how adorable I look, laid back like that. I continue,
casting off stitches, wondering what will be lost if anything gained,
as the rows continue and we increase— (You'll look great in
aubergine, with white shirt and blue jeans), but then see, in the
middle of the back, one long mistake. Should I allow for it, like
the Japanese, who prefer a flaw within perfection, or should I rip
the wrong rows out and make it right— (That's what I'll do), as
I look for you, Mon Chevalier, in black & white, sitting now at
the *Prima Donna*, waiting for your stunning face to make me feel
like one, while the wind chill factor drops its drawers and I must
rev my appetite. You say, "I can always eat." You have eaten alone
all over the world, and you don't mind, but I feel somehow,
humiliated, incomplete, watching the door, thinking of how you
have licked my plate, how good it is just to sit beside you, as you
do your late night calculations, or just to drive and sing you to
sleep, to see you alive, like a little boy with gun and knife, my cave
man, first day of the hunting season, blood on the handle of the
door, the ten point buck in the back, eyes glazed, as I look at the
days, impossible now, without you. For in that absence, I would
bleed, like that carved carcass, of the once perfect (flash of feeling)
night's wet forest, slaughtered there, bleed for the complications
of my life. My father was right when he said to me, "Bad relation-
ships usually continue, they just drag on, until you meet someone,"
but then when I finally meet someone, you say, "I think you're
unconsciously using me, to get out of a bad relationship." So what
are the choices, Dad, where do I eat. Things aren't always so clear
cut, and I know you simply want to stay clean, though you bring
these fresh cut animal organs into the house. The heat of the body's
barely left. I will avoid blood food today, but have to acknowledge
how sexy it looks in the white sink, the way the testicles slowly split
and spurt in the heat of the oiled pan, the kidneys' curve, my eyes
wide open, as I look at you devour this food. "Squeamish," you
laugh. While confrontation pulls up the drive. The deer's heart,
still pumping inside me, hot, like the throb, I hold for you— (She
takes the flesh, she rinses the plate.) I continue to row with purls

and knits, your photo tucked in my airplane ticket. I pay my check, I pay the price. But minutes later, out on the street— You appear, half-smashed, my knight of relief, wearing something around your neck, that looks like a medal, our communion cup— You taste the world and never give up, while I lie down on the bed and cry, because I am terribly, overly tired, because I try and give too hard, because of the lifeless grand animal, because of your love now, leaping, fleeing, because of the things you do/don't say, because of the number of nights and days, left to us, dwindling, because bone cancer comes into the world and builds in the leg of a young girl, because tomorrow will arrive, and I'll be going, and you'll get in the taxi and tell me to think of my marriage. What, my love, are you thinking of then. Are your hands all clean? Whose breath do you breathe. Whose mail do you believe in. I could keep you smiling, keep you young. Will you like this vest? "If you made it," you said. Will winter fit? "I'm embroiled," you said. And who will you kiss when the New Year comes. Who will you take in the deep white snow. Will I ever shut up? Will you continue to listen. The compulsion to say it— slips out of my mouth— and you know I will, I'll keep saying it, suddenly, kissing you, because I believe, in the power of love.

On the Scent

*"it was on his body that I
discovered the odor of mine."*
                — *Françoise Sagan*

I bless myself, I enter in, and smell the scent of nectarine
you named. My juice, the smell, is that of you, I thought
for only in my mouth, your cock, that's entered me
did I first taste this fruit.
It is as close to you as I have come this week.
These are not days of sense, I seek
self-love, and pick it up amongst the rubble.
Listed and wait-listed. Surely I do not wish
to waste myself, wondering
about the difference in some gentlemen, the sterling silver
and the silver plate that covers up the tin.

The vest I knit, then fixed, at first I thought
it smelled like you
and held it to my face, and coveted the scent,
and tried to make
your presence feel immediate, but then like sudden sickness
knew the perfume was someone else's.
There is small hope, I guess, in drawing up the list
of possible potential, names that could fill your absence
not my quota. Perhaps someday
you'll smell their salt and leather smell
on me and want to cinch me closer.

Last week your face had the aroma of the horses
that we'd groomed, the dust and hot hair of the pore
and like the mud flicks on your jacket, I adored
you and continue to for some odd reason.
Don't let the best fruit drop
upon the field to rot, removing elsewhere.
My house is empty, quiet, calm, and my bed's cold
though I am in it. I don't dislike to be alone
and as you know, prefer my linen.

Your big embrace would be enough for me
its absence keeps me scraping. I wonder if three months
will make things change, in public view, if we'll begin again
in some new way, or what.
I want to make a pathway through
not follow like a draft, another, but the same old version.
So keep the cap, keep warm, My Sweet, thumbs up, duck egg,
I raise my leg, because I want you there, your head
your hair, to bury you in me, because we're never through
with birth, the why and from, just where
we came, I come through you, and so you see
you make me, once again, you make me love
myself, my smell, as much as I do you, Amen.

Winter/Shifting

The sky shifts and breaks into the luminous as the light snow descends and the horses are excited, bucked up by the weather and the frollick of the dogs. We take the roadside by which we often go. Their hooves are equipped with resistance, borium for gripping, notched harder than ice. You turn and say, "Another peak experience," and I answer, "We've got a range of those."

Somehow, on horseback, we get into this— The future. Your sense of that exaggerates the already basic understanding of not knowing what tomorrow will hold: (You've got plans.) The quest for some other perfect woman, you deny you are looking for— Some Kathy, some Joan. I believe you should cancel. You say perhaps you might. But suddenly my heart feels the chill.

Now that I am hurt, softened by uncertainty, you want to kiss the distance in between us, reach from your tall mount and take my covered hand. There is something destructive, yet erotic in all this. "You've got the upper hand now," I admit to it. "I've always had the upper hand," you laugh. It is partly what has drawn me to the geometrics of your bed, totally at home in your circumference. But how far can you expand to embrace me, as you have, and you do, before you turn to make some chick and leave me stranded. I am inching out on ice to a fire that's burning. I look up the meaning for *delude*.

You take off on your tall horse, racing up the road. I try to hold mine back, working to control. The light swirls all windblown with snow above the pasture. You say you are ecstatic. I acknowledge, "What a team. The Ecstasy, The Agony," humored, I am cared for, and the moment's mood has passed. The sky shifts and opens— Perfect timing takes you, as you once caught me, spread upon the high mound of pine needles, waiting for the springtime mulch. That season seems so far from this white covering. Dormant, virginal— You said you'd take me in the snow. My whole face turns beautiful before luncheon, shining like this winter sun upon your brow.

I too will want to walk off the wine and conversation, but will give you what you need, time alone. Later, we'll take that toboggan ride together, fast, down the long chute of our love. Now we slow our warmed up horses in the snow pure woods, forget about all future weekend travel agent plans, that might take you to some mule-faced bed. For you are riding just with me, and that's the way I like it, that's the only way to honor what is precious to us both.

You will give me your lecture, like a lawyer, then your love. I will take your advice, dear, while the pine boughs shake their load— Take your hand, as I have given you mine. But will you wait the time it takes to part the past away? Will you always be my future horseman? We'll unsaddle in the closeness of the stable, blanket them, and turn. I will rinse the silver bits in fresh warm water. You will take me in your arms, while outside, above— Beyond, the agents are all floating, waiting for the sky to shift again.

Ashcroft

Our two paths ran parallel in the moon-bathed
boldness of the snow field, as the high range rose up
parting with its darkness, into the thinnest reach of air.

I moaned as I moved and couldn't speak to you
as we slid down the trails on our runners
separately, together, getting there
home, where the mountains at last melted undercovers
and the moon became a wafer on the tongue.

With your sure warmth above me I felt the white peaks
softening, giving way to the awesome
effect of your touch. I recall now
the beauty of such stillness— How we entered that immortal
place together, and came back to pitch love's small tent.

Yet what returns with this memory of the mountains
above all need for human kindness, ascending
from their earthly pine-held folds
into shivered whiteness, is an aching
for eternal reassurance, out of reach.

How strange it is, I feel
to be alive like this, in a love that keeps us
grandly apart.

Cupid's Hunting Fields

Cupid, you blinded fool, look where you've got your foot. Right on some poor girl's pussy. I know you must feel for your victims, the ones who have fallen for you. But it also must make you quiver, the message referral desk answering service, suggesting warm testable flesh. They want to be struck by your arrow, Sweet Cupid, though maybe it's your turn to lay down the bow, come forward without your defenses.

I felt it that night at *Marcello's,* a certain tremor in your hand, a delving in your look, as if you had a secret plan for me. I believe I belong on that treasure map (marked with an X), for only you know where my jewel cache lies. Oh take me to Italy, darling, and lay me on a dirt bare hill between the grapevines. Let the sun be as hot as we are, let the leaves expand their dark promise of bouquet.

But that was one night in a million, and I'm just one star in your sky. I swallow that time release capsule, and ponder— Did you even pause to taste the soup? I eat you, I read you, I dream you even. Last night, you were naked as a fawn, falling backwards over the bannister. I caught you by the ankle, very hard to hold onto— and then suddenly you were lying way down there. I just gaped and admired your enormous balls, blooming like hibiscus flowers.

Sometimes you remember that I mean something to you, and surprise the corral with a hug. Loving me like that, I melt from behind, into an endless go-on with you. Though I can see now that you are panicked, about a lot of things in your life, left as you were for a younger man. Will the Godmother grant you your wish, be your type-hunt replacement, so that you can keep up the myth— Eternally youthful, seductive, Sweet Cupid, let loose upon his hunting fields.

You were disgruntled last weekend, when your love life refused to form some perfect plan. Even a thousand fast phone calls won't make it. For we have to restrain ourselves sometimes, otherwise the flesh of the face takes on this decadent look, which is the only form of aging I am sure of. Yet I know it's hard not to indulge yourself when the game overflows the wood.

I want to undress you also, have you hold still long enough, so that my memory won't blur. Just slip off that armor, Sweetheart, that golden breast plate you wear, secured by a ribbon, the color of blood. You can part the crossed rag that binds your eyes, place your weapon on the ground, believe me, this arrow won't hurt so much. You might even come to like the way it feels. Turn to me now. Take my sting. Then fall for the first real face you ever loved.

The Fawn

My love is like
that wounded fawn
I found
lying
in the wet ferns.
I carried it home
in my own arms
and its scraped neck
bled, on my white
shirt,
I wanted to try
and keep it alive
to nurture it some
and then return
it to the wilds
where it belonged,
but as I stroked
its soft neck
and fed the wounded
warm milk—
My love died in my arms.

Relapse

It is over,
she thought.
But it is never over.
Even when there are no words.
Even when the stars
strain against the sky
to get there it's not over.
The world does not begin and end.
Neither do our lives.
That is but the fallacy we call for.
Even as all love goes on forever—
What the human heart can barely
grasp. And so when I can not reach you
I will not succumb to the pointlessness
of pain, and summon up extremes, but float here.
For the love I am calling on is buoyant.
Her waves are but a relapse
of bliss, relief,
washing up and over
before the silky retreat—
And there is so much room to hold you.
Even when you can't be held.

Up Until Now

My birthday approaches with a build-up of dread. I weep on the phone and curse at the guest list. Where is it I belong, should I send myself flowers, and prepare myself for the worst? But no, I must stop the little youngster who follows, the twelve year old daughter of my worst disappointments. I rescue her right at the edge. Then both of us are glad to be born into April, cruel as all birth is, hard weather of risks, that first flowers must suffer or bloom.

I wake into my lover's arms, and know it is a perfect day. I can barely wait to begin it. He hums down my body and my instrument deepens, the resonant tremor of lips as we lay. I slip off to set our table in the sun. The cool fresh air enjoys my lungs. Holding the little heart he hung around my neck, I kiss its silver smoothness.

I wonder if he knows to what depths I am grateful, for the colors of caress and the zillion tiny eggs that are encased in each shad roe. One can't help but dream about babies, for its always much more than the material thing, and I have to save room for the cake. His sweet dark cake, the single stalk of candle lit, is thick, like him— He sings, I wish, then blow— We eat then smoke, and link our arms to drink champagne.

Everything reminds me of something, and it all leads back to the inner egg, which stirs and awakens to him. He spreads the camel hair blanket on the lawn, and covers my mouth with moist kisses. I tell him that he's got me going again, and he moves to unzip me, most subtle of gestures. I suck his dizzy fingers right out in the open till I'm out of my mind beyond memory. Oh take me slow, for this is the only present paradise I know, on the high high hill in the sunshine, listening to the tones of ourselves entwined and so in tune, and even when I go I do not leave, or leave off loving him.

What He Likes

He likes, a soft egg, a willing woman with a strong head. A long ride, and a short haul— Let's face it, he loves to ball. He likes to sire a statement, take a pose, to slip through hands like a bar of soap, lost in the liquid. He likes to be contemplated, not pinned down. He likes a little *umph* to direct his food, to improve his palette, to have a plan. He likes being a man. He likes to soak the tip of tobacco in a glass of cognac. He likes pattern, knowledge and anecdote. He loves to laugh, to look just right, to drop asleep, not be disturbed, until he turns to rise on time and give her enjoyment, which he does, to feel her fish flip over the edge. He likes a complication of his own devising, a cat-like eye, encouraged by color, a slippery something. He ignites a ready fire, and he doesn't mind being pulled onto the carpet. He likes, to use his mouth and tongue, his hands are to work with. He likes grapes and gallops and girls. His mind unfurls to the tight tactic. He likes to recognize the symbolic phallic, to see it straddled. Great labels on green bottles. He likes to tease her under the table, to feel the possibilities of cumulus rise, to make her moister, to remain as always, first person singular, to feel protected at the same time, to circle around and be collected, by his best companion, who certainly adores the radius of his ration. This is the balance, which includes his absence, she longs after— He likes to be the first and the last chapter.

Sequence

O.K., she thought, pin the medal on me, dear. The medal of great restraint. The one awarded, to the one who shouldn't be confused with anyone who gives a shit. "If you want me, you're going to have to rape me," she announced, "because I'm not going to seduce you anymore." Her desire became like a turned prophylactic, waiting the weeks out, fear. He always sensed that he had a good fight on his hands, that he'd met his match, his witness. But she had turned the lock and thrown away the key. Her mouth was shut, no kisses. No dentyne break poor baby. Embrace the pain, walk out to it. She squeezed through that portal and was back in the realm of dignity, upright, not looking back to see he wasn't looking either. He was picking a hoof, smart guy. But he liked to be the master of any form of denial, and this form excited him most. (*Scream,* and no one will hear you . . . *Run,* and no one will care.) Fire on, lights off, music on, clothes off, no the clothes stayed on, while he poured her some brandy, gave her strands of hishi, which she tossed aside, and told her that he really loved her. "Sure, and I loved the dog I grew up with, too." She unbuttoned his shirt in a careless way, "Don't try anything funny. I'm just playing with you, using you, because your passion's no longer convincing." With this he was determined he would have the bitch, and he seemed to rise higher, expanding above her, that gleam in his eye, as he descended upon her, but her knee went up and stopped him. She strained, as he easily forced her both knees open, long enough to press his whole length between them, but she turned her head and her lips were shut. He had both of her wrists in one hand now, holding, pushing her pants down, her velveteen pants. She tossed her undulations as if she could throw him, wrenched out of his grasp but he threw her back, and she slid to the floor like a snake of music. He grabbed her hair, shook her once, kissed her, and at first she fought that goddamn mouth of his, but he forced his tongue and his hands were all over her, opening her, feeling, and she thought of peeled stalks, oil smooth and glistening, voluptuous breasts, slippery as moonshine— She was sinking down into it, for a moment, submerging, but caught herself— Wait— she was pushing him off her, and he caught her foot, tripped her, then tortured her, ha, with the slowest of touches. She pleaded, she squirmed, in the wreck of her outfit, flipped herself over like a fish on the road, and beat her little fists against the blood red carpet, and he had to chuckle some, she was such a rascal. He flexed his skill, keeping her held there, then yanked off her pants and threw them toward the fire. She had a high firm ass. He was about to abuse her. She was calm for a moment, just lying there, waiting, but then she burst ahead — He wheeled up and caught her, dragged her to the bedroom and flung her on the bed. She seemed reduced to some kind of creature, moving back towards the corner. He could take his time. His smile crawled across the extent of the covers, while she cowered, shook, and when he touched her — She screamed. But he smothered her with silence, he buried her body and she died for him, not knowing whether she should cry or laugh, but she knew she was his as he polished her off.

Even Too Much Is Not Enough

But neither is too little. When he's good, he is very very good, but when he is bad, he's disgusted. Irritation is his middle name. So she balances on the middle of the see-saw, waiting for extremity to jump. When comfort comes to him, he destroys it, then looks up wondering where it went. If she's cool he can't stand it, and acts totally concerned, giving her kisses til she warms up. Then he can grip the steering wheel like metal. He wants no partner, only anyone. He wants her out of his life now, because she's under his skin, and no one's allowed that closeness. He says, "There is no other woman in my life," but next weekend he's invited one of them. He is neither going up nor coming down, like a child on the wrong way escalator. He wears a lambskin disguise, and thinks his name is cleared, because he can describe his worst qualities. Everyone has something to say about him, and he has to hear the responses, like a cupboard gulping up its own cans. She is his constant replenisher. She makes him more real than he actually is. His rules were always clear though his actions spoke otherwise. He wants her to come, to go away. She must be some kind of receptacle. He says that this lack has nothing to do with her. It's him, it's Only Him. He wants her to take the butter from his bread, the cream from off his coffee. He tells her she hasn't any judgment, because she's taken up with him, and she answers he must have a lot of self-hatred. He assures her that he's very fond of himself. So then he must also lack discernment. He is a lady's man, who prefers the acknowledgment of men. He is kind, but then suddenly brutal. Insatiable, yet always on a diet. Her friend writes, "You must need this relationship, because you were married for so long. Men can change, but generally it's too late in my opinion. You'll get tired of the hurt, and you'll leave." Still, she wonders if he'll take her with him. For everybody needs a vacation.

Holy Mackerel

It seems too soon to say goodbye. Tears bound up and you warn, "Don't start," but I think— You're always going, as your hand waves out the sunroof. Two hours later you call for me to come, for who else could you take down such fast rushing water, over haystacks and holes, just your tall drip of laughter. And when we dock the rubber raft on dry land for a moment, I try to fix the velcro of your codpiece, kneeling on the ground, and the guide yells out, "We don't have time for that now." (And I got to hear your laugh exploding.

I live for my small explosions. I would die to live again in your arms. But suddenly we're back on the highway in our fast blue cars, flagged down by an hysterical patrol man. Taken in tandem, you plead for a discount, while I giggle behind both hands. Driving on, side by side, giving looks to each other, like— Meet you in Great Barrington, baby— your naughty little tongue that makes me boil over and churn like "Big Nasty" in the Hudson.

I'm going along. I'm up for the ride. Moving beside you as if I belonged. And when I feel you looking toward next weekend's menu, I know it is only false hunger, that I'll meet you in the stable, and no one will see us, as someone reads what's written in your guest book— *Love from Addie Infinitum.* Because what we have is like the limitless blue we galloped beneath last weekend, we lay under there, right out in the sun, when I stroked your face and believed in us.

I would keep your pillow always close to me to smell. Sleep beside you for the rest of my life. Holy Mackerel! I liked the way you liked the idea. But this river rolls hard when it's high and full of danger, soothes when the current moves slow, and I offer you this raft where you can float over boulders that twirl you in a dream of spinning motion, or you can head right for impact and get thrown— Doused, cold water flooding down your wet suit.

I prefer the fresh washed warmth of your body, coming to me again after pasta. But we're both off now— You to heavy business, and me to the blue grass of horses, pink dogwood in bloom. I wonder when I'll see you again, working as I do on the future, knowing you're on top of the present tense, flexing your mind like a muscle, though you need me to buckle up your life-preserver, unfasten your safety belt.

Possibly I trust too much in these moments we have, so ready with my basket, like a not-so-little Riding Hood, for the Big Bad Wolf is in the woods. I have given you all of the contents, my edibles, the sweet meat of my heart, and I know you could devour me also, in the guise of a reliable love. You're a bad bad boy, and I like you in leather, and I'm never ever bored by you, or by the way your fingers work, the way you brush your hair when I'm about to mess it up. Remembering the tiny pine bedroom where we slept, "Just big enough for one," meaning us.

Final Proof

Business might be bad, but *she* wasn't. She wanted the whole wide world to be his. No need to impress her, she felt she wanted to please— Beside him on the smaller horse. Her hair was bobbing with blond curls, the evening air was like liquid, and he admitted that he had gotten used to her. His caramel colored sweater was tied around his neck, and she couldn't take her eyes off him. Or watching him stretched beneath the oak tree, she wanted for him that ever-reaching fullness, wanted music to pour over him, the great big night to enclose them both, allowing the picture to develop— The one of him naked in the vegetable garden, towel tossed aside, exposing his great physique. She hungered for every solid inch of him, so why did he worry about those bits of himself, as if preparing for another's judgment. She wanted him to spend the whole night in her bed, allowing herself to lie spent, recovering himself in her presence, amidst the morning light sounds of the river. Was it enough that he always returned? That he turned to her often enough, "*Je reviens.*" But when other couples spoke of marriage, their second or third, he eyed her oddly from poolside, as if pondering what it was he might want. He felt comfortable with her, like the best of shirts, made of the right material, and he desired the strokes she lay upon him, like cashmere between his skin and the world, assuring him, always reassuring, that he was her champion, the man of her imaginings, that he *would* succeed, the most handsome, the best, the sterling key to the lock of her tight sex. He said that she was "his girl." That tickled her fancy. She liked the sound of that. So why was he reluctant on the telephone. She never knew when his unexpected tenderness might come, perhaps a loving stroke, or a kiss before the others. Somehow these little moments soothed her. She just wanted it constant, and believed his luck would change if he only stood beside her. He said that he already had, but she knew that was different than being jerked out at the last, dashed into motion come Friday. Did he need her in turmoil to test it? Wasn't her existence for him, complete, enough proof? She was hurt that he hadn't seen the fireworks with her. It took the life right out of the spark. He almost forced her to take up with other men, because it seemed to excite his interest. Shocked by the list in his telephone book, the numbers of available women, and she wondered what sort of fool she was to hold him so singular in her life. Maybe she would have to move away. Maybe she was just there to sustain him till a better time, when an even younger woman might go looking for a ring in his driveway. Still she hoped for a breathing enlargement, a sky that could deepen with ever-shifting clouds, towering before the downpour, then mingled in the warmth of the earth, growing in the garden, working hard at the desk, eaten from the plate at their table, cleaned and stacked and straightened, before sailing after luncheon — For he took her to the woods. She took him in her mouth. He took her with his tongue. She wanted him to say it, and as she came he did. Oh yes he did (he does) he did, and forever in the present he was hers and she was his.

The Good Time Is Now

He reminds me that the good time is now, that we're together riding in the last light of day, and the air is filled with the exhale of flowers and the earth is green and moist. I feel such tenderness towards him, as he approaches his fiftieth birthday, protective of the child in him, the unborn thing, that comes to life within the kisses of my mouth, until he is a man and takes me, and dies the most familiar little death. I know now why this birthday hurts him, as if the years have not amounted to enough, though affirmation is his riding partner, and fifty is a kind of view. He remarks upon the soft olive green in the marsh field where the deer bound away like passing time, alert and afraid, with no intention of ever killing anything. He rides down the slope in his khaki shirt, the one I'm wearing right now, and I turn to look back up towards him — The softening sky is all a humid rose, and I think that he's the most handsome. He has learned that my love won't annihilate. Both of us, suddenly grateful, to see this awakening of earth life together, to witness the dogwood, alone, at the bottom of the path with its constellation of blooms. To me, he is just as wild and beautiful, as that tree floating solitary, still. A warbling fills the air, this time of night this time of year, and his birthday to me is a blessing. My man, with his shoulders shifting, as his horse descends. My man, with the thick, warm fingers, covered with dirt after planting. I wish he'd rub them all over me. Oh, to feel the drive of his passion, the power of his mouth, to make him feel as young as he actually is, not defeated, for this is a beginning place, and I'm dazzled with belief that the good time is now, and that it belongs to us both — Stunned, as the yellow of the mustard field, we galloped beside that evening.

Speak to Him

First night of the fireflies—
those lightning bugs of brightness
seen like transcending stars
clustering near earth,
and as I gaze out into their darkness
their momentary flickering says— Speak to him.
Tell him that you didn't mean it.
That you're sorry for being so frantic
and so rash, that you never really wanted
to diminish it.
Humble yourself a little bit.
Let him know that you're still there
even if the time for him has passed.
Let him know, that in truth,
you've been constant
only wrung all around the wrong way.
Be calm now, like the lake under midnight.
Let him know that the water is quite warm—
that it is safe.
Let him know you'll understand his decision,
that the need doesn't have to be so great.
And if it's possible to swim a ways further,
the moon will surely rest
lightly on his shoulder.
Tell him how you'd love
to hear his voice approaching yours—
Like two brief hovering lights
searching out the darkness.

Swan Song

She believes that she wants it, her swan song
with him, her extension towards one more delight
of an evening, one kiss and one utterance —
Last chance at a calling, but why long
for the song of such beauty
that's dying, why strain for the trumpeting
call, her failure at living,
for she has descended the scale
as the swan's neck goes down, undulant, breathing
its last, and she thinks of her death and the world.

She has sailed low into the last note
of evening, the tone that folds over
like paper, the whiteness of white
swan's wings, with the life all gone out of them,
breathless, Ah —
It could have been otherwise, the swan song
composed just for him.
Not the compromised man,
but this mate of her mind,
the one with the sweet smelling arms.

She sees him as separate, inviolable,
yet still she would come to his bed,
dressed in the white swan's nightgown, all lace
shooting from the shoulders,
a bouquet of redness
in the room, hearts hovering about her.
She would aim her arrow
just as close as she could get —
But somehow, it punctures
and the air seeps out
as she drops her robe and there is nothing.

Now she comes close to earth
with her unearthly singing —
Hushed, but still throbbing

the air with her wings,
as the soul of the lost swan moves out.
Gone, with the clouds frothed in moonlight—
Off into the chilly air.
Freed now
even from her song,
her sad but most beautiful song.

Inner Everest

I too am ready for the journey, but am going nowhere. Staying so still, how far will I further. Alone to you, will be a relief, no telephone calls, while it frightens me, this solo, no matter how much is arranged. The difference between us, staggering, as if holding hands were a contradiction. My long trek will be descent, and not towards elevation, unless by going all the way down, I accept what I've been running from — What you've been trying to tell me. Yours are the Himalayas above. Mine, the Himalayas below. Grasp this, my love, with *lo & behold,* last kiss then let it go. May you let the mountain enter, sink deeper than you have made possible for me, to open you, make real the moment in its present tense, as you forgive the mother, The Great White One, indomitable, forgive the wife, the sister, the inappropriate lover, forgive the feminine trap inside, that unadmitted sufferer, to feel the fear that one must gain in order to welcome it — Precious. That gemstone spat from the earth, your life, to know it is worth the effort. Not to run away, again. Not to cut it off, as if it could be found elsewhere. Forgiven for giving so little, forgiven for living too much. I climb down the slope into darkness, for each step taken upward, into the light, the snow. To ask that the difference be mended, that alone and separate, we each be made more whole.

★

Easier leaving than letting go, but rising at that early hour, I felt honored to see you through, driving past country fields with the sunrise that first of September, where the mist fed the river and soon the city was near, and then your departure was nearer — It crept up into my throat like a physical thing, and I fed it sweets and smoke. I touched your hand, your thigh, your cheek, waiting in the airport lobby, from Newark to Nepal. You were in the best of moods. They had bumped you up into first class, because you are a first class guy, and you took that to be a good omen, just as I did the two fawns, picking their way through the pasture, the afternoon before, as we saddled up to see the sunset, galloping, holding hands, down the two paths made by one vehicle. And it hit me that our summer was over, just as it began to hit you. The import of this take-off. I announced, "I had better go," because soon it would overwhelm me, and you walked with me to the exit, took me in your arms and kissed me. No one has ever dared to make it so good. I watched the clock in the car, down to the very last minute, as your wings rose into the air—*May the mountain be kind to you*. I take your flowers home. I take your basil in my hands. I take your memory to my mouth, over and over again. *These* are the words that come.

Love Notes to an Impossible Person
(1986–1987)

Love Notes to an Impossible Person

She was just plain gone on the entire person, and could barely keep her hands off him. There was something majestic about him, gruff, yet humorous, playful, yet tough. He was solid as a brick, "My Hunk." Ready to fight if he saw someone's weak spot, it made her walk on raw eggs when she could run like the wind, and he saw that this quickness led to moving ahead to a future where he didn't live. He interpreted her kind of emotional speed as a desire to control or possess him, but really she just wanted to direct her own life and needed the reins of a relationship. She pictured him more like a tortoise, deliberate. She could bang on his shell and he wouldn't pick up the phone. She asked, "Why am I crazy about you." He figured it was just the lack of men in her town, or that she was addicted to his version. Indeed, she was passionate, and he wanted her too, and that might have been the cause for their recurring explosions. "You really know how to fuck up a blow job!" She repeated what he'd said, as if she could get a hint of what she'd done wrong, but it was metaphor he had intended, that the weekend had been perfect, so pleasant together, and then she started to get sensitive. The more she came to care, the more he pushed away. He didn't want a woman to need him. He liked to hold her tight. She enjoyed the pressure he applied, but wanted to soften him some. He believed this was something to beware of. He was the first man to ever make her sweat. She was a fearless woman, but scared to death of him. She loved to see him laid back on the pillows, gripping her breasts as she rode him. It was hard not to tell him he was gorgeous, and when she did, he said, "Right," as if he didn't believe her. He was athletic, a champ, but an "inside boy." He was oral, but didn't like to use his mouth. He had the most voluptuous lips. She considered him the best kind of meal. She could have feasted on each part for hours, the strong, broad chest, magnificent arms, delicious balls, his hair was almost auburn and luxurious. She loved the way it smelled. He got pushy when she didn't want to talk, some crime. Can't a girl just be quiet in her misery for a moment. But no he would threaten that he'd take her home. Ten minutes later he'd be perfect. A bad puppy he was, impossible to train. She had to hang up his towels just right. He didn't want the pressure to have to perform. She was flexible as well as demanding. He liked her lavishing attention, but got antsy at a point she had yet to respect, the kiss upon the back of the neck spot in public, the digging her way under the sleeve of his shirt. "If he doesn't call tonight, Mom, drop him." He didn't like her singing in the movies, but liked the fact that she could be outrageous, a tomboy with a life of her own. He had an amazing cerebral capacity, but needed to move out of that safety, into the quarry of the heart. This was like pushing a cat into water. Perhaps he needed her feelings to float. He was a man who enjoyed the shared freedom of men, though he included women in touch football and was exceptionally nice to her dog and her children. This had endeared him to her from the first. Still she wasn't used to the kind of punch he packed in making a mere statement. He didn't intend to be mean, inconsiderate, it was just that his work must come first. She could see how his life tipped out of balance, but he would refuse the right medicine. She felt that she wanted to be monogamous. He thought she should do exactly as she pleased, so that he wouldn't have to be responsible. Sometimes she felt that she could simply do no right, that he was aching for a way to get out of it, while she yearned to encircle his back in the night, to talk and laugh and enter the depths of each other. He just had to create this aura of disaster, then rescue them both in the boat of his arms.

Frame

Yellow apples hang on the bare black limbs, weathering frost and snow, and now this freezing rain that washes away all covering, and still they hold, persistent, like someone who won't give up, grasping lost time as a punishment. That tree once dressed for the future. So much to be had for the plucking. It kills me, the waste of it all. The waste of fruit and heart. I've confused pain and longing with love for some reason only the crib-cage knows, little fists scrunched up like withered apples, the big red heart of the baby inside, punched until it collapses, until it turns brown inside its skin and comes to tell you this story. Why are they always excused, the boys who belt apples at the barn. Why am I tired of holding. I just can't try anymore. I walk to the electric fence in my mud boots, feed the horses who lean with their hunger. They crunch up the apples "gone bad" and I want to believe they are grateful. But when will the apples on the boughs in the field, somewhere between your house and mine, when will the golden apples fall, since no one, obviously, wants them.

Here in Heaven

If I adore you, you must be adorable, right? Like a flamingo perched on a truffle (with a wish), or a taffeta tux on an overstuffed bear. Now that I've seen you in action, I'll never put pressure on you again. Right? I'll just keep sending you postcards, each one stamped with a silver hoof, the mark of our good luck in love. You might never be able to say it, but I feel you coming closer to the surface, about to burst through into the new air of light. The scarf is just as long as you are. Designed to keep you warm as your arms keep me. Forty-four seems harmonious, well-balanced, a good year to even the portions, while my laundry hangs out on the line in the snow. May this season survive with us within it, as I close my eyes, and you are there beside me— How I love to hear you talking in the night, when our fingers come together, clasp and I'm in heaven— Just hug me once hard before you go. A grey squirrel now leaps from elm tree to limb, bouncing snow from the branches, while the trunk stands still and so does my love. I want to make a nest out of the covers, acknowledge that the bed smells very well fucked. You excite me so I sometimes want to slap you, to challenge the strength of your nerve, but then I also like to see you resting comfortable, hear you chuckle when I whisper, "Who's the sweetest boy?" You have truly become my one darling, but who ever saw an angel smoking a cigar. It might disturb you to hear about "sentimental value," or to look up and notice your own picture by my bed, but you've crept into all parts of my house now, including the bloodstream. Don't let it make you nervous, it's a fact, white as winter, as surely as the years make you crow, because actually you *are* getting younger. Right? So now that your birthday has passed, our tickets lie ready in separate drawers, waiting for reunion at the Fairmont. Surely I'm amazed, "We didn't even fight." Here in heaven, anything is possible.

Return Flight

Are you wide awake as I am, tonight. Unable to get used to the
time change, unable to get comfortable without an arm to get under,
or a panel of flesh, back to back. You're probably in a deep dream
right now, making yak sounds as you sleep. They needed a hard
hitter to get the job done. I need to look forward to your return.
The red suspenders set right across the white shirt, your brown
eyes amused over the tops of your glasses, as you dip your head
and chatter on. I liked her response to— "He's brilliant,"— So what.
Frankly, I don't mind being dumb, going riding in the rain along
a road I've never ridden on a horse that's more brilliant than mud,
even eating (stupidly) an unripe olive (bitter!) and yet knowing
I'm in Paradise. I was. Yes, I like the smart way my skin feels after
that kind of chill and a stint in the outdoors hot tub. But what's
best is coming home to bother you some more, subject you to the
onslaught of affection, until I steal a kiss and receive the welcomed
crush, for love's the most fortunate accident. If it lands on your
doorstep, don't regret it. Even if you feel you don't deserve it—
Accept it. For all we want to do is breathe, deep breathe, and I
believe in romantic resuscitation. If given the chance, we always
spring back to life with even greater tenderness over Pancakes
Oscar, before dashing from the car in the rain, and miraculously
arriving unwet. (I still insist the weather was perfect.) I love to hear
you wandering on about art, while I follow on the living carpet,
right up to the swan hanging down the dark green door— Don't
forget what polenta is made of. Now that I'm back, I keep pictur-
ing that print of the quadripeds, the rippling fur of those big bears—
Powerful, primed, together forever. I'm glad you understood how
much I'd miss you.

Crazy

My darling always thought he'd like to be a sex object until I made him into one. Now he thinks of strategies of escape before he dares stir in the morning, how he will pretend to go brush his teeth, and then quickly pull on his levis. Seeing the disappearance of those muscular calves is like watching good wine being wasted, wanting more kiss than compensation, wanting his rough morning face in my hands. I lunge when he calls me, "Meshuga," though I know he could throw me right over this bed. He has come to accept my fawning, my can't-keep-my-little-hands-off you, and I'm used to his pushing these gestures away. I just find him too irresistible. He answers that all the women he ever dated did, so I cuff his hat and feel miserable, which leads him to anger and unkind words, "I can't use this aggravation in my life anymore." I suffer a spell of insomnia, that lasts until 4 a.m. Thank God he understands the subtlety of my longing, "If you don't fuck me I will kill myself!" I also recently gave up cigarettes, and agreed to on one condition, that my kisses would taste sweeter than apples, and he'd take a big bite more often. But now I have noticed a gradual falling off, and when I confront him about this, he pops miniature marshmallows into his mouth. I'm too young to be replaced by junk food. I'm too old for unrequited love. The snow has been falling for ages, and he's like someone who was built to hibernate, and I'm blamed for keeping him awake. The thimble is a humble symbol, but I'd rather pick the canon or the horse. He says something about my being a banana, and my mind slips, and I think to rip his shirt off, just to get a whack of his skin, but instead he holds me down, whips out his army knife and snips off a lock of my hair. If he were Italian he might at least have kept it, the way I'm tempted to save the wads of kleenex he inevitably leaves in my bed. Even such remnants affect me. His pheromone's my one cologne. I think we were made for each other, an exchange of crazy casseroles, if only it were the dinner hour and the spoons were back under the covers, especially now that it's supposed to snow forever and I'm editing this collection of erotica. Sometimes I wonder who hung the terra cotta angel from the ceiling of his bathroom, and where went all the women of his bachelor's past, and how will I become one any different. He tells me how there's no one he would rather see, but how he truly dreaded coming over. He seems to say everything in two directions and the intersection is my head. I know he will have to leave me, intending to return, but maybe I'll be buried in snow by then, lost in this winter like his underwear in the big white mounds of his mind, snowed-in by him, this man who has driven me crazy, sex mad, snow blind, approaching irrelevant, because he wants to break me God dammit he does, because he thinks I always want things *my way*. Pot call the kettle black much? Suddenly, I just stop caring, and then he's all over me. Nothing's wrong as far as he's concerned. All male, oh man, he makes his move, to grapple and to pin me. His physical love's a vise wherein I struggle to return to sanity with him, until I just lie there, smitten.

Frozen Heart

If you think I'm writing up a love poem, you're wrong, for my heart
has turned bitterly bitter. Nothing in life can delight me, for I've
simply had it with winter, had it on a lot of levels. Maybe my roof
won't hold any more snow. The gutters are frozen, and it's started
to move back into the walls. The whole house is going under. While
you, my friend, fly off to Florida, over the longest weekend, leav-
ing me here on Valentine's Day with a heart shaped frozen ice tray.
My seven year old says, eyes brimming full, "I just don't like to
be left behind." Well baby, that goes for all ages, just don't bother
crying your heart out, because nice hot tears only freeze-dry here
and you might get shock-o-the-eyeball. Oh to sit in the shade and
drink lemonade! I am pissed about the kitty litter. I'm tired of turn-
ing on the broiler in the morning so I can bear to unthaw the toast.
I imagine your great big plane departing, and think that your cock
could just freeze and break off. Oh to move back to California!
To breathe in the plum blossoms now. Smoke fills my basement
when I try to burn wood, and I sleep with at least six covers. Still
I wake up with frozen vocal cords and can't say, "Down," to the
dog. My hinges creak with a new kind of sound, for everything's
been affected. I take a hatchet to the spills that cling to the clap-
boards, devouring paint with all pleasure. You think I want a nice
tall glass of Coke with little frozen hearts floating around in it? I
could use a hot one-way ticket. But I'm locked here, I'm stuck —
My agent confirms this — Other people plan ahead. I deserve to
be loved. I deserve a good thaw. I deserve to hear running water!
But I'm mainly furious with myself, for not loving myself enough,
for not doing it for myself again and for waiting around for your
frozen heart which departed with block ice you.

Strange Streams

She enters his life with her children, "The Plague with her two lit-
tle plagues," I mean, descends upon his 30th floor apartment, where
he'll suffer this insult of contact, worrying about apple cores festering
in the garbage, for she never lets up, stuffing notes down his brown
gloves, "I love you," in the right, "You love me also." She has to
introduce the idea, so that he can get used to it, as he comes to
accept her presence. She likes watching him stroke her younger
son's head, or strolling up front with her eldest. He's just one of
the boys, slipping noodle-like out of the kitcheny-grip of all women.
He dreams of a massive lasagna, that wants to devour the world.
She starves when he refuses to partake in her, for he would prefer
an absence of smell, while she is constantly "with him." Moment
by moment, he is present to her. He insists that he doesn't need
anyone, as he walks with her boys beneath the giant sperm whale
in the dim blue, ocean-lit room. Later he refuses to make love to
her, because he's furious that she wants him to. All she really wants
to do is cuddle, see his teeth shining white in the dark as they talk.
She would float on her back down the length of this river. She would
have him by her side. Her hand is open to him. But he's afraid
he won't live up to his own fabrication. She can't love the Real Him
which he doesn't show anyone. Still, she is stunned when he dresses
in the morning, but it ruins her day when this woman calls . . .
Does he think she's just a dumbass schicksa? It's as if she carried
around this Christmas tree, and as soon as she sees him
approaching— She lights up and glows, "Forgive me for being
jealous." But he's flying ahead through the great museum, show-
ing her sons all the armor— Swords men used to fight with for
their lives back then. Now they use other kinds of weapons— Deceit,
overwork, and emotional distance. She wakes up and recalls strange
streams, the place where a body's been buried in a wall, the actual
seam where she could cut to get at it, but she doesn't have a damn
Caesarian's chance to rescue her corpse of muffled feelings, the ones
that will blow to the surface like spume— "It's Over— That's IT—
I'm getting out of here!" Two minutes later they are making love,
in the deep blue parts of the ocean. She'll drive back to the coun-
try and collapse there, truly thankful that she wasn't born a boy,
and though she thinks that her sons are terrific, who wouldn't, she

is grateful for this singular sleep, that he will call her in the night, that she has a tape machine, and can listen to his voice over and over.

If They Can Put One Man on the Moon,
Why Not All of Them

I believe that I smell chemical— cigarettes and perm— as I walk
into the odorless garden and pick this poem. Sadness pervades me
totally. It enters like a seed and blooms, a colorless rununculus—
I detach and carry like I've stolen something— for it was your
garden, you were scaring me out, but I hold my lifeless treasure,
as if I have damn well earned it. We each walk into the world,
aghast, as the gift of self-punishment lashes back. Good feeling has
fled, it has run from us, as I carry our see-through rununculus.
I even resort to shaking the 8 ball, then stare at the "definitely yes."
I picture a girl child alone on the see-saw, bouncing in a kind of
agony. Will I always succumb to impossible men, as if trying to
prove I'm not lovable, winning again what childhood presented.
Could trophies like this be repeatable? I can sob on the doorstep
for the loss of you, while a girl-friend assures, "*We* are family."
Her lover waits inside. You can make the same mistake countless
times with predictable partners. And so could I. Better to suck on
old smoke than to hear you say "No" when I want you. Wielding
it away with the power that's yours. Even the night won't deny this.
But I can't seem to replace the breadth of your shoulders and ache
for real life as I'd reach for your chest— you pushing the heat
through my body. How did I change for you suddenly. Why does
nobody come to me here, where I sink in the dark. Why does
nobody pick me up. Do I scream for the milk that would make
me sick, dash the cup with all kindness? I too am utterly broken.
Stored, like damaged goods, and we know how much *they* are worth.
To hell with it all, just another obsession— one of the nerds of prey.
And I've got a flock of those, trapped in my net, banging in the
chest for nicotine. To thrash together, pain within pleasure, or to
simply walk away. I should give up a lot of things and get on with
my life, singular, solid, stinking. But I'm standing on this side of
the fence, where the flowers refuse, sprouting colorless. I know about
your middle name, my love. Funny how it complements Laura.

Incidental

Forced into writing by that tyrant, rejection, unable to produce the unconditional milk you sucked from your mother, still raging. Having two boys I must lead through example, and *this* is no example. People are not incidental. Love *should* come first. I can only hope my boys outgrow childhood, and will someday come to love women, through one, otherwise— What good is anything, what worth is the coming of spring or success on the mantle. Who cares, frankly, about the penthouse or boat. When desire goes stale, and I hear you don't want me, I turn against myself but then stop it. You'd dash the demands of a thimble, so fuck it. I had no other choice but to walk. I will not be clobbered, again and again, and feel it can only get worse. So why is love hopeful? Is that the core of its power, or would I continue to delude us both. This must be the most brutal time of year, mid-March, ruin laid bare as the snow melts. It's as if I saw my life there, broken on the ground, and we've troubled the heavens enough.

Never Trust a Bachelor Over Forty
in the Fast Lane

She didn't want to be pregnant either. She knew what it entailed. He didn't. He didn't want to change his life. Said repeatedly that they could never live together. Right. So why pretend that there's something building. Why these little gestures, if that's all it amounts to, like junk mail stuffing her hopes up. Or would his warmer feelings surface some day, be a male kind of love she could count on, and once he had "figured it out," as he said, it would be permanent, solid, like he was. While she was more apt to push on— "If you can't go to Italy, maybe somebody else can." He took it as emotional blackmail, though she had been thinking about her son, who'd been studying the Renaissance anyway. He suddenly suggested that both children go. She told them, excited, but then realized— What kind of vacation would that be. And as it turned out, he wasn't serious either. He wanted to pretend to be a father, maybe one night a week, without having to go through any shit work. He could buy her sons underwater watches, or a model of a Lamborghini. He could take them all out for barbecue ribs and drive over 100 miles an hour, and not ever have the kind of fear their father might have, in some other house, in town, hearing of it— How there is no controlling the heartless.

I Hate Your Guts

I am hopeful, forgiving, as I bring the red tulips to your weekend house, leave them where they will look beautiful to greet you, "For your two lips," I write— for your lying, fucking mouth. You cancel on me and my children. You tell me on the phone how you took the flowers out, because there were ants crawling over them. Well, the ants weren't from my garden, baby. And now that you're gone, cold-cocking this weekend, I flash in-an-out of there to get my vase, see the flowers dumped over, dead. I was hoping that they had survived you, but it appears that nothing does. It just reminds me that something naturally lovely, can be abused, go unregarded by the thoughtless. I thought, "I can wait for you," on Wednesday, but now you can stick it in the mud. I know your brute rudeness has little to do with me, but I'm tired of my own understanding, tired of saying, "I'm not mad, don't feel guilty," pretending that none of it matters. You don't call when you say, taking every gesture for granted. Well the taker has taken his fill. If I never see your face, it'll be too soon. I'll grant you the same, like a blessing. Astute enough to realize you're ruining your life, but it's no more than a self-fulfilling prophecy. Do me a big favor and pretend you never knew me. Don't speak my name in public with your fraudulent lips, and I'll do the same for you, believe me. Sure, this anger's the flip side of all the love I felt, dead as the flipped over tulips on your table. Throw them in the garbage, or have your girl do it. I just wish they'd never opened up around you, or given you one real moment. Ants, black ants, from your woodwork, your walls, crawling and breeding and busy-busy-busy, shall be your most likely company. May they work into your sleeping brain, and make your bed their dirty laundry.

Dreadful

You must be the black bat of my bedroom, jerking entrails of the underearth with you. When I flick on the light, my siren center of disgust makes me crawl, head down, with my blanket, for you'd drive any woman that way, down and out, while your too-smart sonar allows you not to touch her. Oh most horrible creature, even when I conjure you in human form, brutal and shuffling, with the awesome weight of potential lurch, with the brain of a flying rat — You have used the human heart as your plaything, for feelings are loathsome to you. Yes, you delight in making love cower. I run to my son for help. He descends with the name of a warrior, cheerful to be on the hunt, but by the time he gets down, the thing's been murdered by my friend the cat. Still, I can't sleep with that under my bed, with its black guts popped, and its wings hugged up. My enormous son in white underwear amazes, how he can collect this dreadful thing for me, drop it on the porch in an old raggy apron. Now I can sleep without fear of you, tangled in my hair, catching on my dreams. Bad love can be the worst addiction. But I'm weaning myself. I am truly cleaning house, and soon I won't even stumble on the thought of you, like the splat of a mud pie that suddenly swoops. You with your bat-like vision, unable to connect, unable to really look— No, I won't let you descend upon my daydreams in the name of terrific sex, which was really the oppressive monologue of your one-way control. I click off the light and hear the river running on. That's the kind of man I want. Long and lean, steady and comfortable, one I can sleep with through the slumbering night. Yes, I have swept you out, sent you back to your mother in the cave-sucking earth. When I shut my eyes, you're just a shudder without substance, a blotch upon my heart.

Looking for the Exit

I might be free, white and twenty-one, but I'm still looking for this
man I love, as if over the expanse of a crowded space, but I can
not speak or reach him. I could spend hours at this, getting out
my telescopic lens, examining his wonderful biceps, the color of
his boyish hair, his lips, the smile that bursts into sunshine, then
retreats like damaged weather. I know I have hurt him, but he's
hurt me too, and I want to put an end to prolonging it. Yet I'm
faced with this armored tank, and can't break down the defenses.
He's put me on hold to airport music, while I consider the difference
between the dancing fuchsia and the dangling bleeding hearts,
strung in a line like our losses. "What are we running from!" I
yell at my friend, who's allowed me to bring my pain to his
barbecue. He explains the Jewish neurosis of looking for the exit —
"If the act isn't being pulled off, or if emotional alarms start ring-
ing, if you remind him of mother, and he feels trapped, you better
believe he knows which way the door swings." But I can't quite
believe he wants out, not yet. If he did, I could never keep him
in. I just don't want to look like this new abused leather, even if
I picked out the finest linen in Florence and this Italian underwear
with him in mind, even if I want no other. I thought I could win
him back with my gestures, the thoughtful gifts that were carried
all the way, the postcards, the poems, the emblems, but now the
words seem to evaporate, now that they've been sent and read. Have
I made no imprint? Do I need an epitaph chunked out of stone —
Hey baby, I'm crazy about you! I keep this fanatic hope, that
because love endures, it will work out somehow, but maybe I haven't
admitted, that I care a lot more for him than he'll ever care about
me. This friction can not be relieved by mulling over the flatbeds,
even if the aroma of earth and moisture under heat feels like a kind
of promise, and finding his bracelet like a second chance. He wants
me to try not to touch him, but his hand felt so firm in my hand
that night, and now he's become so distant. I imagine him seeing
me from across the room filled with people — how we are drawn
to each other — how he'd grab me in his arms — kiss me until I'm
unconscious, or until I wake up, and go out into my yard, fill the
twenty plastic bags with the piles of needles and leaves that have
been heaped along the driveway. It feels good to take care of my

entrance. I care about this long way in. I imagine how he might drive up at any moment, remain a while, rest and read the papers. I remember us in a better time, lying together on the sofa, squeezed in like two morsels of pleasure. Sometimes, it was more like a big white blanket wrapping us together, or a fire inside with a roof under rain. He recalls the impossible parts, and I feel stripped of all effort. Nothing left to offer but myself now, and my life doesn't seem worth much. I've tried to come forward, to meet him halfway— I have waved my flag of surrender. If he says he wants to listen, he should hear what I say— Don't postpone my life any longer. It's spring. It's May. Can't you believe in it? Can't you say Yes for once? Because I'm still planted in your first row, magnetized, adoring, not even conscious of the exits, until I see you heading for the closest one, hoping you will turn to take the entrance.

Beyond Divorced
(1987–1988)

Car Pool

I left the house at 11:30 a.m. in order to run errands, leaving enough time for the half hour drive to Monterey for my 1:00 therapy session, over at 2:00, giving me thirty extra minutes beyond the half hour drive back, to stop at Taft Farm and Jenifer House, before picking up Ayler at Degarmo's. Clovis gets out of school at 3:00, and was going to get a ride home with Jud's mom, but by 4:00 he still wasn't back. I called Liz, and she said that the canoe trip Jud had taken with the 3rd grade class hadn't gotten back on time. She had been at school, had waited for an hour. Clovis had left his backpack and jacket in her car, and was happy to hang around, but then Liz had to leave to pick up Samantha, who was dropped miles away by the high school bus. Liz came back to school and Clovis had been sitting in some other car, wondering where Liz had gone to, but Liz thought he'd gotten another ride. I explained to her that I had to leave by 5:00 to take Nathaniel and Clovis to South Egremont for little league practice, and I wanted to feed him beforehand, since I had to leave at 6:00 for my real estate course in Pittsfield, forty-five minutes away. Lilan, who lives with us, would stay with my children. Luckily she had her own car. I packed Clovis a dinner, collected his uniform, picked up Nathaniel and drove past school. Still no luck. So we headed to South Egremont, where I explained the situation to his coach. On the way home, I drove past Liz Gershen's, and she said that Ann Elizabeth had dropped Clovis at French Park. It was now 5:25. I flew in the direction of North Egremont, to find Clovis lying alone in a field. Clovis didn't want to get yelled at— It wasn't his fault. When I pulled into our driveway, I had fifteen minutes to eat. My car smelled like smoking rubber. Lilan arrived from work and I took a thirty second shower, before jumping back in my car with a cup of black tea, racing the back roads to Pittsfield, hoping I wouldn't get stopped, glad to have found my calculator, which the teacher described as "a tool." He said that the math was at the sixth grade level, but I could barely remain awake, and when I got home at 11:00, there were no important phone calls from New York. Sleep, anyway, felt great. When I awoke Ayler said to me, "Come see something cool!" I followed him out into the yard, and there was a dead opossum on the lawn, lying on her back, neck broken and gashed, paws folded in the air, tiny baby opossums littered all about her, one of them half-tucked into her marsupial pouch, still moved, like a thumb in a wound. Lilan, who wants to be a vet someday, came out and saw that all the tiny babies were still just barely alive. I had lost my appetite for breakfast. "What should I do with the mother?" Lilan called from the yard. I realized now what that high chortling sound had been during the middle of the night. Lilan picked the body up by its tail and dropped it in a bag in the trashcan, then collected the babies in her t-shirt. She thought that she could keep them alive. That the boys would help keep them alive. Great, I thought— Nine little rat-like creatures. Lilan walked through the kitchen with the babies in a basket, and I felt a mild disgust for their tenacity. I announced that we had to get going, my morning to drive, off down Green River Road to pick up Jud Gershen, taking the dirt road to school.

Time & The Right Time

I'm thinking about your turning thirteen, flattered when people seem astounded— How did you manage to pull *that* off in so little time— but wait till they see you, Clovis, my boy, who's outgrown his 7th grade teacher, and stands equally tall with his Dad. I wonder if you'll be able to forgive me, when you look back to this year, and see how our family was broken, though you appear kind in your acceptance and strong. It seems like no time ago, when you were born amidst the hyacinths. I brought home a potted purple bulb recently, so we both might remember the sweet scent of your birth. Maybe I wanted to make this your best birthday, because it was the worst for me. I remember my parents were travelling, and they didn't leave a present or send a note. Teensie Brumder and I went shopping (without luck) at Bayshore Shopping Center, and after losing my brand new wallet with the thirteen crisp ones in it, we managed to miss the bus, which made us too late for the movies. Ethel was screaming. I didn't blow out my candles. I can still feel the cake collapse, when my parents returned empty handed. So now I'm taking you to Italy, a kind of promise to us both, that we shouldn't wait around expecting things. When you were born, Easter fell between our birthdays, and now we'll hear Easter ringing by the Arno, feel the whiteness of Florence rise with all remembered Aprils. I've never been to Tuscany before, but feel like I'm waiting to recognize the fabric of a previous lifetime, a fine red cloth perhaps we both once wore. I will toast to your manhood at the Jolly Hotel, your favorite word these days, "just a little jolly money," and when I think to write advice— Be honest, be open to feeling, even if it brings you pain— I'm really hoping that you'll advise me also. No doubt I would have trouble hearing it, like— *Hold back, Mom. Just cool it.* No one sees at first what we are made of, iron forged hot until Mars linked. I lose patience and you request a punching bag for a present. I want nothing but the simple words, the ones that have not been spent. Oh Clovis, all your life we've been travelling companions, but this is our first real trip, first time since you were in utero. No one loves an Aries like another one. Who else could keep up with our impossible schedules. And for you, I see a big life beginning. I feel lucky to have been there from the start.

Broken Home

The world breaks down in pieces. I'm standing in the kitchen, talking on the phone, when a glass jar bursts and oozes, unable to be held, the viscous, excess, olive oil— Or lying in the bathtub, I distinctly think of him, when a mirror falls and shatters. And now I wonder when the case of *me* will crack and break again. Will I contain it, on the stand, say yes and yes to all the lawyer's questions. When he brings up our children, my voice grows quiet, small. We do appear cooperative, yet undeniably broken, after almost twenty years, that number monumental, like some slab stone, split and fallen. We go to *Friendly's* afterwards, and you pick at your fingers. I remind you how you always thought that rash was caused by me. We have not done this to each other. We do it to ourselves. I cry when you get up to leave, and in the car, I cry. It's like the oil that can't be stopped, and I put on my shades to hide, for I have yet to face it. That you are there, with her and glad, that I will live alone, and yet I'm pleased to see the lupine on the far side of the garden, beneath this late May rain that soothes, the timeless baby made of stone with green growth all around it. Our lives stretch back together, but now this fork has split, yet still I know your driving. And when I take your car, it's odd, but so familiar. Stranger still to hear my nickname used on her, and not to mind, to like my own arrangement, to realize your comments, irritate as always. I pull away from anecdotes where I can't share the humor. My love life's like some rumor that you overhear. You were my first full man, and now we've parted, apart now, caring for our children, amazed by them, without regrets, for any of it, darling. I know it isn't final. That we'll go on and no. For even when it's over, the shards combine again.

Far Be It

Sometimes you have to pee *bad* at the beginning of a hayride, and sometimes you are giving a poetry reading and you hear someone laugh, and so you, the reader, chuckle also, thinking you are pretty funny, but the laughter referred to an incident in the hallway. Sometimes the most welcomed experience is when the dinner guest lies down on the sofa and falls asleep. Sometimes everyone else in the costume competition is awarded and you keep returning to the table of the judges, wondering when they'll notice little you. Sometimes you don't understand your own lack of patience regarding the small boy who is your son, and who is crying in his bed for no reason, until the next morning when he's obviously ill, when the log is found rotten white with fake weight, and the guts of the pumpkin's like snot that won't wash, and sometimes the radio blasts off at 4 a.m. announcing world disaster and then you dream someone guesses you are 75 when you are half that age, but don't look it, and sometimes you'd prefer to wake up without the aid of bouncing bodies, because sometimes the hole you dig isn't deep enough, and you figure that your life is just something you have to live with. Sometimes, when all the leaves fall, you can see that much further, but then you notice how far away you have moved.

Weekend People

X called me Thursday, left a message on my machine, asking if I wanted to ride over the weekend. Friday I went to the movies with Y. He is my pal. X introduced us, after I left X for Z. Z didn't call until Saturday late, but after talking on the phone for fifty minutes, Z decided it was safe to have dinner. We ended up having a great time, but he didn't want to spend the night, because he hadn't "figured it out." On leaving my house, he asked me what did I think. "I think this is our last date," I answered. He stormed out of my place, "You would say that!" So I dialed his home and let it ring and ring. He almost killed himself getting to the phone in the dark. I asked if I could wake him up, knowing he would say, "No!" But he said he would call me early, by eight, and then we'd go out for breakfast. By ten a.m. I was in a foul mood. I'd been awake since seven, and nothing. I was getting out my galleys when he finally called, saying he'd been talking to a client. We met in town, but both felt rotten. We proceeded to implement impossible patterns. He wouldn't take a walk. I couldn't understand him. He whined that my phone was always busy when he rang. He escaped to the city after breakfast.

X and I were to have luncheon at Y's. Y had an old girlfriend with him, named Karen. Y told me that he was afraid to sleep with her out of a general fear about AIDS. X called from the highway, saying he'd been in a flood. He was worried about missing luncheon. I said I would let Y know we'd be late. "Just don't ignore me," I told him, knowing he was interested in meeting this Karen. She said to X over the prima vera salad, "I guess I've never seen you at your worst." X answered suggestively, "You've never seen me at my best, either." X said that Y and I looked good together. Once Y wanted to get something started with me, but I protested, "We're friends."Karen asked about X's country place, and he insisted that we all come over. We all drove to X's in our separate cars, and I overheard Y asking if we were still lovers. X said, "no," that we were just friends, just like Y was with Karen. After Karen and Y left for NYC in her car, I said to X, "I bet you have her up here next weekend." He said that she wasn't his type, which I didn't believe, but we had a nice ride together anyway.

I sat down and called Z this Thursday. I missed his voice. I missed his brain. I missed his incredible body. At first he was sullen, didn't want to talk, but then it came out, he was angry. He ranted and raved until he made me cry, so that he could feel guilty and pull away even more. "Gee you're such charming company," I said, forgetting that he wasn't even with me. I mentioned how I thought we'd get along better when I was no longer in love with him. I said how things had improved with X when we were no longer in love, how we were just friends, and he yelled at me, "You were in love with X!" We obviously defined the word differently. I told him that he was devastating, meaning it nicely. He said that if I wasn't devastated by him, I would soon be by somebody else. I couldn't believe we were doing this, or why I was crazy about this man. Y came up early this weekend. He had left his car at X's house, and asked if I could give him a ride over. On the way to the car, Y told me about the luncheon, how X had told Karen, "I'll call you," every time I stepped out of the room. If I did love Y for telling me this, it would certainly ruin our friendship.

The Lily

We had a deal, right? Who abused it. Who chose to ignore the
abuse, and furthered it, who. You see how these things go, when
you don't deal straight, when you use somebody who loves you.
And I did love you. But now, now there's a stench in the garden.
The gardner says, "Dry blood." We had a deal. I was to be your
girlfriend, composing your flowers as only I could. In exchange,
I'd take the arrangements home at the end of the weekend, like
leftovers given to the guest who cooks. But then I showed up late
one Sunday, and the bouquet I wanted was gone. "Did you give
it away to that woman?" I asked. "Don't be crazy. I have nothing
with her." The next time your mother asked for them, though the
delphinium were already moulting, the tiger lilies beginning to curl.
I still continued performing. I wasn't even going to be your weekend
date. I was weary, growing very weary. But I said I would come
if I could, and make a flower arrangement. You were going to have
another big party. Almost every weekend, a party, important people
to please. I didn't feel like pleasing. I went into your garden in
a hurry, wanting to get the job done. I was having my own small
dinner for friends, and I thought I'd pick myself a bouquet to replace
the others, above. I left you the dinner plate dahlias, because I
know how you like their extravagant size, as if they measured your
sex life. I brought my own small bucket, filled it half full with water.
The afternoon was hot, and I liked being up on your pine covered
hill, how the slope ran down into sunlight. I walked through the
garden, gathering, and then saw the lily, pink and white, a three
part flower on a bristled stem. It grew close to the ground, spotted
and fragrant, tucked away. I would take it. Your caretaker had
been threatening to leave. He figured he could talk if he wanted.
"What do you get out of this, four day old flowers in dying bun-
ches. What exactly is the net worth?" I dreamt you took an ax to
your caretaker's neck, that he was walking around with a bloody
gash where the neck joins the shoulder, cutting him off, cutting
all of us, who care for you. I took the lily quickly, cut it low, and
put it in the bucket in the back of my car, hung my fuchsia col-
ored robe over the seat to hide it. I was hot and went for a swim
in your pool. By the time I returned, my car had the scent of
heaven — All that I deserved, cheated upon, just fungible goods,

186

so easily replaced, by a man who needed his flowers around him, telling each that the others meant nothing. At least the *nothing* was true. But I was the best and I took the best. Wasn't that appropriate? (The weekend people arrive— I'm caught. The gardener writes you a note.) I got the message, the phone call, the word. I certainly heard about it. "Should I bring it back?" I questioned. "Don't be ridiculous!" you snapped like an aging queen. Should I come right over *now* and flagellate myself until I bleed? Replacing the blood that's sprinkled on certain flowers to discourage the lips of midnight dear who also steal into your garden? Once I loved arranging, but now the heart's gone out of it. Hot for a moment the Ice Prince rises from his endless rows and is ruthless. My spots will darken as the days do, but I know that I'll survive. I could have lied as you lie to me— "I don't know what happened to your lily. *I* didn't take it, who knows?" Do you know what happened to me? My modesty, my marriage? Did you ruin it all for your own brief pleasure? You *did* offer me the job of girlfriend. Only now do I know what that means. For even as I give, I steal, what should have been mine to begin with.

On the Mend

We are the damaged women with our solid bodies approaching
year forty. Romance is the cherry pitfall where we land, protected
by a loneliness to which we've grown accustomed. Still, this in-
clination to offer myself, picturing my peony fingered. But what
really got me off was being taken in the sun with my sunglasses
on. My party was like a wedding without a groom. And yes, I
missed the one who was missing. I just sent him a postcard of a
woman by her Weber, a weenie on a long pronged fork, "Honey,
I need your condiments. Love, from your missing buns." I kept
looking down the drive, across the lawn, you know. For him I would
always make excuses. But I'm tired of giving out consideration,
of making my unusual soups and the bed, when he's only going
to go rigid in his armchair as I bend to embrace him, panicked
that I might encompass him again. So hard to give in to let going.
What's the matter with fast food if it's straight from the garden.
I can satisfy myself upon the horsehair mattress, with a feather puff
pillowed in sunlight, take an afternoon snooze without having to
cajole some impossible person. Men think they're so indispensable.
"If he never called again, it wouldn't bother me a bit." But I'm
terrified she will meet my lost love, this adorable woman with her
cooler sense of distance, who jogs in the city with earphones like
he does — They would keep in good stride — She'd keep out of his
way, and I'd be unable to face it, life that is, crushed by the gar-
bage truck of illusions. But then, pretty soon, he'd abuse her too.
He'd withhold sex. She'd come running to me, and we'd form a
nice plot to destroy him. We *can* instill terror, we confess to each
other, we brain, we grow stronger, turn back to our art work, put
sex in its cannister, we swim, we stay limber, we dance and do
flowers, make everything beautiful, we have children, all boys, and
they play in such harmony, they roll across the lawn, and we pray
they won't grow up to be your kind of men. To deny the woman
who loves you, brings power. To love her in return, yields freedom,
how frightening, to loosen that grip on yourself. So this gardening
girl put in the guest room suffices to validate your manhood, O.K.
I slip the caps from the berries and make the juice come forth, while
she tells about her latest obsession, how he approached her in wool
socks, how he stood there, talking and flirting, polishing her boots,

her cowboy boots with his foot. She irons my outfit, including the lining to the pockets with precision. Of course she's a designer and makes comments that kill, picturing Ole Big Boy with his Savings & Loan haircut, with his vinegar wine and label stuck on his accent. Even I come to applaud her terrible remarks, which are not unlike baked beans left on a lawnchair. I deep-drink Campari, get hysterical laughing, while moths, big as men, beat against the window, bumping with their noses, pulled toward our light. Don't they know we will have our revenge? We won't be the only ones wounded. By our marriages, broken, deserted, hearts stepped on like beer cans, yanked up and throttled— She even lied in Emergency, "Oh, you know, I was falling off this ladder, uh, backwards," and now she requests just one chicken wing. I see her across the party with pain between her eyes and wish I could be more than one person. Instead I keep looking down the drive, across the lawn, wondering when he will appear. Pain is but a strawberry dropped in my mimosa. *Euuu,* he is surely on my shit list, as if his face were painted on, his announcement a product, his personality just ordered from some catalogue, how he turns on the smooth stuff like sex talk with a faucet, but he has no control over me anymore, and now that he knows it, feathers fly from his mouth, cherry pits, projectile— (That big wrinkled old bruised looking flesh stick, TOUCHED, a nice shiny huge silver dollar in exchange. HEY, let's get-out-a-here! RUN, jump the hedges pretend we're on horseback, the backyard means safety we're home in our girls' club.) Oh yes, he's undone me, left me sprawling in the grass, taken me any ole way he ever wanted, but then one night I could no longer breathe, you know. I just couldn't lay my head on sponge rubber, and the windows wouldn't open, I was suddenly awake, got up and got dressed and got out of there— BREATHING! We can dance away naked in the moonlight, sweet sisters, for the fireflies are out now over the pasture and the river meanders. "Who needs it!" we holler. "Maybe I do," is uttered . But to hell with it, *Hell,* we'll do without for a while, until we are healed, for false love's a cure we can not endure, in this present condition, on the mend.

Why I Never Travel Light

I remember you being like a deliberately slow car, with your right-hand signal blinking. When I try to pass, you take a sharp left turn and bash me off the road, calling it Jewish Law Tactics. Now being in this airport brings a longing for you back, as if I were returning from a funeral, and can't believe that you're gone. A friend of ours played you in a tournament recently — How I wanted you to lose that day, though once-upon-a-time you had me totally in your hands, like that feeling that comes before the perfect ace. I was slain, indeed, I still swoon inside, though it's been months since you mastered my bed. I can say mean things, but not mean them. A truce waves in my head. Maybe failed romance, caring way beyond reason, is terribly outdated, language from another decade, back when they just used gut and wood. So look at us now, are we happy? Or just better armed with our modern materials, so used to each other's absence, the ache inside almost feels normal. It's not. Perhaps it doesn't matter if you win this time. It's all focus merging with the body, knowing that your forehand is a weapon you could use. You always hit *me* upon the sweet spot. They say a little anger makes a player like you better, while it makes me do things I regret, like giving you back the hat filled with horseshit, tearing Ayler's picture from the door. I want to forgive you, so that you can forgive me for simply being myself. Here in this airport with Ayler as he plays, revving the wheels to his "masked vehicle," getting it to shoot paper across the table, because I've asked him to be quiet for a moment. I let him wander off to the game room, though I'm afraid if I don't pay attention I could lose this child. I have lost so much already being thoughtless. I do miss hearing your name at the end of his prayers. Maybe I'll start saying it for both of us. I would ask that we all be protected, renewed. I would ask for a new kind of vision — Starting with the wide white X of the field gate, open to the pasture in moonlight.

Whose Arms

I wouldn't trust a woman who didn't have girlfriends. Even if we do end up talking about men, settling back into the unlit living room, after a Sunday of grilled bluefish, conversation drifting like wind on the wet leaves open to the summer porch. We talk about the Great Kissers. "Hard to find, these days." She tells about her one big passion, how he also turned out to be a run-around, dating the expensive ladies. She cooled it by quoting a novel, that hit the head and he faded. I say, "Why not approach him with postcards. They always work for me." She admits that he was perfect in many ways, she, who's unaware of how perfect *she* is, as she lowers herself into Billy Boy's pool. We both like to sleep alone though, the privacy of reading, lights-out at the exhausted moment. I tell her how my last two lovers didn't like to be touched on entering sleep. I never slept well with either. The tension was a kind of absence that couldn't be filled with enough. Not even orgasm would do. I heard about this one guy who gave his girlfriend thirty for her thirtieth birthday. That sounds to me like punishment. I'd rather abuse myself over him — I'd go back to him in a minute, my impossible person, though I think like some kind of hardwood, he's grown deeper inside himself, pushing protection outward. Still, my memory hungers. "I never turned away from you," he said. I care for him more than it matters. Does he wonder, like me, in whose arms he will end, or if we will ever resume? She says, "Maybe by midwinter, I'll send my great kisser a card," though she read the relationship early and ended it clean. We relapse into forgiveness. Because we are mothers? I fear in my love for my children. I fear that my ex will woo them into his brand new house, with his solid relationship, though I helped him move our old box springs up the stairs, since she said it couldn't be done. He added, not quite nostalgic, "The bed where our boys were conceived." I wondered if it were old ache or new bitterness, when he tossed back my wedding ring, that most familiar weight that would no longer fit on my finger. It was the day they were moving in. Different sheets on our once shared bed. How long does it take to get over it. We retreat to each other, we women, as if seeking nurturance, and it's true I admire breasts. I would fit myself with a pair of them, get you down on hands and knees inside me to hold them up. I ask my friend if she noticed his biceps in that tank top over lunch, what a decent body he has. "Yesss," she grins, "I happened to notice." He still can look good to me, brown from working in his berries. I am one of the varieties. I tell my friend that I do believe we'll both remarry someday, and she's assured by this assertion of mine, though I have a more severe knowledge, that I'll always be alone, or feel that way, that I'll never love a man who'll embrace me, when suddenly I recall, and tell her how I always went to sleep under my husband's arm, how we always fell asleep like that, lost consciousness together, a couple, and I could see us in that bed of ours, a normal double, see us, as if hovering over our togetherness, looking down at our bodies in that warm room, and on our breathing, married, and I covered my face and sobbed before her, as if imagining a past life over— Bereaved, I see, my one, inconsolable, gone, best friend, was him.

Loving My Boys

I have to be careful in loving my boys, to do so with distance, as from my desk, where I sit now, hearing him bellow, gleeful, as he drives the tractor and his full young voice bounces against the forest, the edge of which he cuts. My big boy, as tall as I am, with his twelve-and-a-half size shoe— I watch him in our Levi jacket, as he takes his lariat and ropes a chair on the patio, returning a call from "Wendy." He's got a date tonight, my baby, only thirteen. My friend, Francine, says he's going to be a killer, with that look in his eye, and he's got the meat already. I like to push on him to feel the playful resistance, the teen-force in him, ram-like. He walks into my bedroom first thing in the morning, looking for his brother to shoot. They kill each other, over and over, using red and blue ink that dries without a mark. They drag each other across the lawn, hoist one another from the downstairs up, by an ankle on a rope. My younger son is still innocent enough to come crawl into bed. I gather his warmth, his blondness, into my arms, even hug him in with a leg, and often we fall back to sleep that way, arms around each other's necks. Soon, he too, won't be able to come to me, tenderness met with a shrug, "Oh Mom!" They will be loved by many girls. I was simply the first. They both have heart as well as head. They both will undoubtedly devour sex. But leaving the nest is never graceful. My applause holds back as they tumble and wave. I know I will have to let go, the hardest act— Pretending to turn away, as if I had someone better to love. And it is already beginning. This summer my eldest flew off to the Tetons. When he returned, he had veins in his arms, the way a man has muscles and veins. My younger son *leaps*. I imagine a baby. They will go into manhood with their good bodies, confident, ready, whole. Take life on and plunge it. Make it thrive and yield.

Revenge

The dog has been trying to kill the cat for over a year now. What I didn't know was, the dog was serious, and at last I believe she's succeeded. I met you a year ago, tomorrow. What I didn't know, *did* hurt me, that you were *never* serious, but it won't be the death of any of us. I will have my revenge more slowly. I see, at last, my intuitions were right— So afraid you were of your double life entered, while I stood there innocent with desire. You abused my love. You abuse my love. I withhold the curse that could cure my anger— *May your two balls fester and ripen with blight!* No, the Truth is my revenge. I know you are in great bondage, dragged by the horse of your own dread past, desperately trying to fabricate somebody we could believe in, but everyone knows you're your own worst enemy, that you can't shut up because you have nothing to say, nothing, really to give. I know it was never your penthouse, that she pushed you out, but it hurts that you pushed me away, with the excuse of work and then ran to her. I still feel abandoned, and don't understand like a child hit smack-hard for no reason. I give my dog killer an egg. And remember how quickly she took to you. You still invade and disrupt my sleep, make me incapable of decent love. Just how much time to get over it. I picture you screaming with collick, driving your mother crazy, as she drove you, changing your outfits hourly. Did she keep you so clean, you went out of your mind at the touch of a woman, hovering in to amend you. Poor baby, grow up, poor boyfriend, arrested, poor dead to the touch, poor wrist pulse, digestion, poor power play paunch, poor crossword, tossed, poor girlfriend sucked into sucking you off. I am jealous as some bleeding steak tossed onto the fire searing! My friends are clearly tired of it— "Wash your beautiful hair of him. He was never worthy of you." But it's still like I whooped in the Triumph that night, with the summer wind lifting my yellow skirt— I spoke the fact that survives us both, that redeemed your bountiful emptiness. "If we were lovers again," you said, as we parked, "I'd never get rid of you." I just wonder if I hadn't been needy, if you hadn't been such a cheap fuck, and had bought the gold chain to begin with, then the heart might have worked, the gondola gone down and the bed born out such fruit. I believe that anything's possible, but not with the made-up love

I use, making you what I needed. My humor misread, crawling into your bedroom, the *N. Y. Times* in my mouth. Now I see why you were worried— "What if there'd been another woman here!" When all along, there was. You're boss of the baddest shit I know. So loving you makes me as low. To rise from it, I release my revenge, turn back the clock to a year ago, and the cat returns, unharmed, I'm glad, that we didn't die, though part of me does, as I say goodbye to an impossible man, and mean it.

Beyond Divorced

As soon as you decide it's all right to be alone, good things start happening. You get the call. From the man with the deep down voice, drawn slow and humorous through the telephone, an enlargement of all you ever wanted. Kind, nice, "Don't use those words on me," he said, but really it's all right to be comfortable. If a man falls in love with his eyes, a woman falls in with her ears, and I did. When he finally arrived, walking across Main Street from the Bonanza bus, I pointed at him, asking, You? He pointed at this other old fat guy ahead of him, and I knew that he would have my heart. From there on our troubles were over. He'd also bashed his head against the impossible and survived. Suddenly all life seemed adorable. I fed him lobster bisque and risked spoiling him. We went to the movies and were the only ones there. I was good and didn't mention next weekend, but he called as soon as he got home, reassured. Can either of us begin to believe this? When he invited me down I was nervous, on his turf, that things would be different, but no, making out on the short couch, laughing through the night with the windows wide open, reaching in the morning beneath the comforter, Oh! Is *this* what it is all about. I knew there were others in the background, but liked to hear his friend say, "They're dropping like flies," and, "Don't let that woman out of your sight for five minutes." Instead, I wanted to give him more time, for we all need silence and distance, and his words rose up in green letters on the screen, melting from page to perfect page. I massaged his sore neck in the theater, then he turned and put his arm around my shoulder, giving me the tenderest of lips. I would see the bond widen, as the lakes of my childhood, ever-embracing, with room enough to swim, no hurry, forever, I could move with this man, stare into his blue eyes, hang onto his bicep, one bigger than the other from his powerful forehand, but I like both the right and the left sides, of his mind and his windows, one curved and one square. I like the color of his leather jacket, and the fact that he offered me his underwear. I slipped them on and thrust the air without worry, for I believed he'd find everything he'd lost, including 16 shirts at the cleaners, including warm chicken salad, including health & fatherhood. I asked him why he was so happy, and he came to embrace me, this amorous man— A current runs through him,

and his movements delight me, as does the song he cups howling
in his hands. I missed my bus, it was cancelled I mean, because
snow was falling in the Berkshires— Wet snow, on the red reach
of early October, unseasonable weather that kept us together. He
called me back into his arms, when part of me thought, don't Bother
him. Instead I took a cab, and sang "The Street Where You Live,"
coming home to his jagged shaped sweat clothes, hanging on his
good firm body, like a skin that is easily sloughed. We were down
to the rough, bare bristles of his face on my neck and his fingers,
drawn down the length of me, at long last, up into the depths and
I gasped. I wanted him to know it was the best I'd ever had, that
I could move out of history, that we could leap into the mutual
perfect of some future tense without terrible tension on our backs.
I admired his cherry wood furniture, the curves of it glistening,
how I could hang onto the arch of the headboard like onto the boom
of a sail as it swings. Am I getting too mushy, too forward, too
me? Will I be allowed to be all that I am? "There's nothing more
endearing than to see an old couple, happy together, talking their
heads off, knowing there is no one else they'd rather be with." We
can both grow up now and stay young forever, where the only crush
we know is the weight of each other descending on desire, "A good
thing we aren't physically attracted, you know." I try not to think
of you leaving, and that I have to go now, off on the earliest bus.
I wake up to winter in Sheffield, shocked, as if I were returning
to a war zone, where you will be sent so soon. Iraq, Iran, he ran,
she ran, they can off together to Ninos. I believe while you're away
I'll want no other, for you've become my guy, my one, though I'm
prepared for any kind of weather, as the snow which felled trees,
which crushed houses and wires, rivers running high a devasta-
tion. The night that it happened my children lay in their beds at
their father's house and heard the crack and rip of branches break-
ing. All through the night nature pruned and went on like shell
shock to the ears of my young. I drove home and began to free
the limbs from their load. Some branches bounced back, as if
grateful, others littered the lawn like past loves. I would drag them
to a pile and make fire. I still felt luxuriously dishevelled from your
bed, melting in memory, and believed we'd stay limber, unlike my
ex, who thought I was lying about the bus. I heard the whine of
old emotions as the attack began, felt the insults of humor and
reached for your warmth, but all I found was your photograph,
pictured in a grainy black and white, almost sad but very very
wonderful, for you have seen the wars and dealt with it. I have

seen the storm's result. But now the stars shine bright with a lot of luck, for love expands beyond our comprehension. What will come will come in time and keep on coming if it can. Everyone deserves what's happening to us. Suddenly I put all trust in the Infinite, praise the grand upswing of life, and thank dear friends, "Why didn't you introduce us sooner!" Sooner *and* later. Beyond has begun.

Serial

He touches her chin. She looks up to the ceiling. The lamp light
is hidden behind him. He is wearing a red and green paisley tie,
another old girlfriend gave him, but he touches her in such a way,
we know tenderness has a beginning. He has joined her now, sit-
ting on the other end of the sofa, eyes closed, cigarette in hand,
as she stretches out in long green skirt and black sweater. We can
see the matching green of her beads and woolen scarf. His hands
are expressive. She is watching the words that form his mouth.
The hem of her skirt reaches the dark grey of his suit, and her feet
are tucked behind him. They have switched sides now, and she's
right beside him, reading a book, "Sex Tips for Girls." These two
have only known each other for eleven days, but already they are
bridging the city and country lives of their mutual friends together.
The book is gone now, casually tossed, and his hand disappears
behind her butt. His other hand seems caring, and holds the out-
side of hers. She likes that combination, romance and lust, and
smiles at him as he delivers an anecdote. Their heads touch. He
handles the beads at her neck, and his father's watch is shining.
He has his arm around her now, and she is slightly lowered,
laughing. She grips his arm, while his hands appear confident
without trying. But he seems tickled, as if something lovely were
happening to his insides. He's teasing the top of her head with his
fingers, as she pushes away a bit amorous. He gets her in a mild
neck hold, and her head is back, mouth open. Suddenly a tender
shot. Her curled hand brushes his tie below the knot. She has
already forgiven him for wearing it. Her hand creeps around his
neck, while he has his hand securely on her lap, looking down upon
her laid back head. She's waiting, succumbing to his well-dressed
advances. Their faces are close now, pressed tight to each other's,
as if the room were pleasantly sinking. He has a momentary look
of sadness, from the past, but *her* face doesn't believe in it. Now
he beams just as gladly as she does, wrapped even tighter in a big
embrace. They turn their heads to each other, and complete the
pose with a firm and equal arm held kiss that keeps on kissing and
the dark grey suit becomes the same one color as her surrounding
sweater while he grips her hard and she holds him to her— Mouths
and hands and arms and clothes— All blend delirious together.

Correspondence

I want you to be reading this, as I make love to your cock. I want you to be standing there, reading this, looking down at the top of my head, engaged in the act of loving you, maybe looking up myself, to smile through half-closed eyes, only to sink again, into the pleasure of mouthing you, and I can feel you getting harder, wanting to push it in a little bit deeper, and I am getting myself aroused, reaching up to touch from your chest, expanded, down with curving nails, to where I can hold the stalk, and lick the tip and kiss your tightening balls. I want you to be engaged inside my orifice. I want you to feel me feel the meat of your buttocks, as you plunge, withdraw and plunge, as you collect my hair and groan— I want it to be so good you want to free yourself in my mouth. I want you to fold this poem, as if you can't stand to stand uncertain anymore, but have to let it go, allow— And let the paper fall, just as I make (imaginary) love to you— Real in the mail.

Love Chant

I want you in me. I want you on me. I want you with me. All through and through me. I want you over me. I want you yester-day. I want you backwards. I want you more now, because you went away. I want you monthly. I want you mostly. I want you totally. I want you day by day. I want you lazy. I *want* to want you. I want you sideways. I want you plenty, babe. I want you sooner. I want you dancing, or maybe laughing. I want to see you. I want to smoke you. I want to treat you, to speak and to have spoken you. I want to serve you and to unnerve you. I want to watch you, then maybe whack you. I want to kiss because I miss you. I want to rush and then to blush you. I want to sit beside, to lie and hold you. I want to nudge and to embolden you. I want to hear you talk. I want to mount you. I want to pounce on you. I could receive you. I want to read you, inside the covers, and in the morning begin as lovers. I want your deep take. I want your net shot. I want your left side, as well as right, hon. I want you in part, and then the whole lot, for you to get the very most I've got. I want you near me. I want you on me. I want you always here within me.

In the Zone

for William Sherman

Barely gone seems too long when I think of you and remember
how you loved me our last afternoon. You wanted me to drop the
bathrobe, didn't you, and lie face down on the bed? It was warm,
like spring, and soft together kissing you, though I started to shake
before the quaking broke through, then quiet with your heartbeat
on top of me. Hard to rise from your arms, though the clock said
go— How could I cry at departure. It was more like the pain of
the implement withdrawing— Only then do you feel the wound.
I was almost in gear, in the car, when you said, "Let's kiss some
more on the sidewalk." Then you did say the words that make her-
his, before you held me goodbye— Now the words fill my head.
It just doesn't get much better than this, and baby, you've got to
believe me. I drove home to doo-wop and oldies but goldies, eating
the kniche as if it were your fine hind end, sweet meat of man,
my William. Being with you is being "in the zone," where all is
on, stroke after stroke. You stoke me, boy, with fuel to give, fresh
fire to live, last bliss to hear your voice on the recorder, and know
I've got a bit of you to get me through. I'll stay in the zone where
you left me, Bill. It will be some place to return to.

I wanted to be the first to leave a message on your machine— Make that little red light go *blink blink blink,* like certain excitement in the erogenous zone, but instead I decided just to listen. For you have collected me like all these poems, and memory keeps its covers. I'll be all right, though we're into October and the Falling Moon. There are workmen rattling in my kitchen downstairs, inserting a heater in the spice cabinet, and you know how I like *hot* food. You would be the only worker in my crawl space though, cranny of sensation, crevice of the brain— But how can I leave *that* message. I have labelled all the days on my calendar, see? Forty days and forty nights, as if an ark of isolation stood stranded here in Alford without coupling. The world was made for twos and you are missing unto me. But these leaves'll let go before I ever do. By the time you return from Bagdad, Bill, the tree outside will expose itself, embarrass you like I do, in bare vivacity— Let's mesh and stick together for the long haul. Meanwhile, I'll keep laughing my tall head off, for the happy heart is no tollbooth.

★

I think about writing you all the time, when I'm not thinking about you. Or when I am, writing, then— I have to remember, Bill! Boy, I miss that guy. Think of it. You in mental starlight. A fresco of Bill, biting the bull— Oh, when will I get serious. Making light, because alone and without you, here with my bowl of borscht soup we bought together on Amsterdam. Sopping it up with peasant French, I'm also submerged, but know I am lucky to have had you, darling, come walking (limping) into my life. Your photograph sent me whirling, a big high in the long day of this here girl, for distance, as they say, makes my lone heart grow fonder, especially with such a sight to contemplate. Mildly melancholy, posed for the news. In brief— I'll stay like a banked coal, which will, no doubt, burst into flame when you touch me hello.

Ah, the guests have left, but loneliness hasn't. Yes, we went dressed for a night as Cupid's Victim, and survived. No, I am no longer wailing, for Time has stopped, kicked out of my sail. I cried, when nothing came in the mail this weekend. Our good friend held my hand in his and told me things that didn't reassure me. (Remind me again, that some men never even pick up a pen, and I'll chill the pang and please it, though my headache rages, and I'm in the stage of anger left with changes.) Oh dear blue eyes, don't risk your life. I'll rinse out all of his insinuation. I feel so linked, as two stars balance each other out. Maybe you've written, and it's in the heavens. November tonight, and nagging doubts hang over my eyes, lids swollen.

★

I did a mail dance and then a sweet rain fell. The box filled with the voice of my beloved, a word that isn't often used anymore, but I do ride out of the storm's horizon into an Indian summer afternoon, on "Twinky" my pink and green mountain bike. We climb the hills. I'm totally smiling, on you there, in Ishtar land. Goddess of love and fertility, also war. We never seem to leave those zones behind. Jupiter, your Sagittarian star, is shining close to the full moon tonight. And where's your arrow aimed, my hunter. I'll go out and stare, cause I wish you were here, hold up my target like a moon that's milking the November skies, while you stand on that other side of this round globe in war's harsh light, getting the footage, to bring it home. I wish you were in *my* cutting room, putting us back together.

You not back now till December, I'm told, from Cairo late night by the river, White Nile, not forgotten ancient scarab, I hold, on-to the thought of our reunion, some time later, see a hunter in the backyard woods, passing before my study window, and feel low, that war continues, all life aging, in hiatus. I'll let that tight fist, jealousy, get bathed in light that's gold and loosened, but I want you back in my arms tonight. I want you here in my bed all warm and ready for a major session. When we come to each other, we come "as is" and I want to receive that person. Both of us flying further in miles, but I know we're getting closer, inch by inch, we're getting nearer, heart by heart, it's growing firmer, hour by hour it's passing over, into that time I'll have with you.

★

When you get home, I'm gonna be in outer space. So bring me down, into your arms — I miss your W vein. I miss your simmered drawl. I miss — Falling for you ever time you enter the room. So now you're in Kuwait, dry as can be, 9,000 miles and eight hours across a couple of seas. You know it's been worth the wait. When you get back, it's gonna be, as if you never left the zone. I've been such a darn good girl. "Have Fun," you said on the phone, but darling, that's impossible, and I won't until you're home. I miss your looseness, and the way you put your hands right under my blouse, kissed me in the bar with your half-drunk delicious mouth. I miss going out for nova Sunday, to bring it back and drink up the juice. I've done enough talking now. I just want to listen to you, close my eyes, and feel your hands, and hear the news that renews.

I reared up and saw my matching half, and laughed the laugh gods love, when human pain has passed, and the barn doors slide to a warmer state of mind, the kind you get when your Man comes home, when you find you're not alone anymore on this hard earth in white December — pipes that froze are running now with water — stationed in the desert, but now he's made it back, following the whinny of the one sweet call which is his name I say out loud. I rise to meet his face, his fur, receive his sure advances, and when he enters through my sleeping hair — We both entwine and laugh the laugh gods love to hear. When we awake, my long long arms will wind around him, warm *and* warm. A lovely morning on our dish will come. Just like the big doors kiss on barns.

Back Together

Two bright pink azaleas in the middle of winter, in the before storm blue, by the window, the waiting, dissolves, as you open the hotel door and enter in. Ten weeks shudder and close as my arms fold around you. Shaking, half-naked, I am overcome. Kiss me just kiss me— Make us bright as the flowers. The rift is now over and you too disrobe.

When your arm broke on ice, your eyes went desperate, young. This fresh fear of aging, that the body won't hold, up under the weight of emotion, that someone younger by the counter could perform and breed better, but new love goes into the mending of the bone. I care for this torn-slung, painful part of you, even if a history acts hard to need anyone.

Anything could happen. Anything could change. I don't deny weather, winter so bitter it offends humanity. I put blankets on the hood of my blue car, sheltered. Anything could alter, now a January thaw. It takes a day to warm us, by three it's hard to leave. I want longer stretches, animals of time. I want to believe, to shuck my maniac brain, that bores us with jealousy. Needless, you say— When pieces knit together, they grow even more strong.

Outside on the corner across from the window-lit grocery, beneath the lamplit streets and the red bricks of Boston, I feel the romance of returning to where our New Year rolled in. I'm glad we missed the movie and can sit here at *Davio's*. I like your three day beard, test the difference in your two arms— Love all that's conflicted and human about you, deep undercover, comfortable as lovers, merging toward sleep.

Wretched love's felt more keenly, unlike this lapping, this lingering. But who can reside within the half-there heart. This hovers gently over us. It warms by the stove. It purrs on the line when you call me long-distance, washes over the windshield and walks the common gardens. It works and plays and pounces. It cries in the night, and comes back for comfort. It takes notice, takes care. The time it takes to heal.

In this indoor city plaza of fine shops, we dwell in the well-lit cave of merchandise on weekends. I am not a fancy girl, but sit beside the fountain and hear the indoor waterfall, forget about the crazy cold weather I'll return to, getting in my car. I have lent you my coat, a big wide coyote, because it covers your sling. You have covered me also, and stirred me to sing. I give you my word, dear, I'll take your warmth with me. It melts the middle of winter, and flowers, unexpected, knowing soon, in good time, all our limbs will wrap around.

Conversations at Bay
(1988)

His Sweater

I first noticed the sweater on the upper shelf of his closet, that night when I couldn't sleep. I didn't want to disturb him, so I tried sleeping on the couch, but felt chilled alone. That's when I found the sweater, a rosy shade of gray, luscious yarn with flicks of angora in it. Not a masculine sweater, I thought, but it got me through the night.

I remember with fondness, the anxiety in his voice, calling out my name the next morning. He brought me back into his big bed, and I think we even made love again. He seemed to like seeing his sweater on me, or it surprised him how nice it looked.

As the weekend continued, I borrowed it casually. Later, I even asked if I could keep it while he was gone. At first he said, no, that he thought he'd take it with him.

"To the desert?" I asked.

He thought so.

But on the day before departure, he mentioned, "Didn't you say something about borrowing this sweater?"

My heart seemed to suddenly open.

"But don't wear it every day."

Once he was gone, I wore it more than occasionally. I even slept with it sometimes. But as the weeks went by, I noticed the arms of the sweater grew longer, and I had to roll up the cuffs. The once tight middle now lapsed into a loosened sag. I imagined it good for pregnancy.

One night I was wearing it, while knitting up a tiny sweater for the unborn baby of a friend, when the phone rang. I knew it was him, calling from Cairo. Sometimes I *know* these things.

He worried about his sweater long distance. It was worth $300, he said, designed by the mother of an old girlfriend.

I realized I never should have borrowed it. I sensed he already regretted his moment of generosity.

Days later I returned home and saw a note scribbled out:

Call Mel. Immediate. Important! I knew that that meant he'd received his visa for Iran. I tried not to seem alarmed, though soon he would enter a country where human life meant nothing, where children were sent to walk across mine fields.

"Now I won't see you for another month," I complained, reminding him that I had to leave for Zurich right before his return.

"Don't take my sweater to Europe," he said.

"What?" I asked.

"Just don't take my sweater with you."

Suddenly I felt alone, with or without his sweater. I knew we were talking about the sweater, instead of admitting how frightened we were.

"And if he gets killed you can keep it!" my son yells.

"I don't have to wear it again," I said, but now his voice was loving and calm.

"I want it to be where it is."

I wore his sweater to bed that night, sort of like having the last word, but when I woke up, I knew I should wear my own clothes. I would go out and find my own sweater. It would be red, with a design around the yoke. This new red sweater I had in mind would be my own chosen emblem, of a woman living alone in the woods, dressed to live, dressed to go on, no matter what. This one wouldn't be glamorous. It would be almost rough, but that's the way it's got to be these days.

And yet tonight, as I sit here warmed by the fire, my feet are growing cold, and I'm still wearing his sweater, for I've grown accustomed to it. It will find its way back into his hands, though it might not fit him now, any more than my over-sized love. But maybe some night, he'll feel the urge to sleep with it. He'll go to the closet and dig it out. He'll wrap it around him, as I have done, to keep him together, and warm.

The Introduction

The first thing his mother said to me was, "*You're* not Jewish."

People always took me for Scandinavian, which I wasn't either. "Well I'm part Jewish," I lied.

"Ma, what do you care."

"*I'm* Jewish," she asserted.

"And how many times have you ever been to temple," he asked her. She appeared to think about that.

"Never," she answered, though she apparently cared. She was in a Catholic nursing home. There was a cross on the wall. She didn't like lying there, and who could blame her.

"You want these people to know you're not Catholic," I said, sitting down, close to the bed.

"Yes," she said. "I'm Jewish."

"So you have two boys," I went on, to put us on equal ground. "I have boys too."

She looked at her son. "I'm healthy," she accused him.

"You have beautiful skin," I told her, and she looked in my eyes and nodded yes. Her skin was very smooth, almost without a wrinkle. Her frail body barely filled half the bed. For a second we seemed in agreement.

It was Passover, and on the way to the nursing home, Mel and I had discussed what "pass over" meant. He said it referred to the Jews passing out of Egypt, but I thought it related to the angel of death passing over. "The lintel of each Jewish household was marked with blood."

"Lentil?" he said.

"So the eldest son would be saved."

"Do you know why we eat matzo at Passover?" he quizzed me.

"Because leaven relates to evil?"

"Because there wasn't time to let the bread rise," he answered. "But I'm not a religious person."

I thought I was, because I didn't care what anyone *was*. I imagined that God found little amusement in all our petty differences.

"I'm Jewish," his mother announced. I had been pleased that he wanted me to meet her.

"Practically all my friends are Jewish," I had told him, "but do you think I've ever been invited to a Seder?"

213

He started telling his mother about his job at *The Christian Science Monitor,* how he was the only Jewish man on the floor. And how weird they were, never smoking or drinking, not going to see doctors, and how they made jokes about Jews.

"I told you," she said. "Didn't I tell you?"

It was like the brown-and-the-blue-eye club. Mel ate pork and shellfish. You can't be sometimes Kosher. Even Catholics ate meat on Fridays now, and boys were allowed in girls dorms. Rules change.

"Did you know that The Last Supper was a Seder?" I'd asked him on the car ride out. Yes, he knew that. But did he know on the night of that Seder, Jesus drank from Elijah's cup?

"I'm healthy!" his mother announced.

He looked at me with humored patience, accepting his mother totally. When he described his relationship to her, it reminded me of mine with my eldest son.

"Do you love me as much as you loved Liza?" I'd asked him.

Instead of answering, he'd responded, "Well I don't love you as much as my Mother." I thought that an inappropriate response. I would hardly compare my feelings for him to those for my father.

"I'm healthy," she said out loud.

The nurse came in to feed his mother, and began with dessert, ice cream, instead of the pea soup which followed, a disgusting progression. Two bites and she cried, "I'm full." But the nurse kept prodding her with nourishment.

"That's enough."

"Come on, Ma," he said.

"I'm alive!" she burst out.

"If we could bring you something, anything to eat, what would you like," I asked her.

"Grapes," she said. "Red Grapes. I'm full!" But then she accepted another bite. After each bite she said, "That's enough."

His mother was not much older than mine, my mother with her whirlwind energy. I doubted if she'd ever end up in a nursing home. She was more apt to kill herself speeding to church in a car.

"I don't love you anymore," she said to her son. "Get out of here!"

He looked unperturbed.

"You don't mean that," I said, more shocked than he was. "You're just mad that he's going away on a trip, and you won't see him for a while."

"Yes," she said.

"We're both going to miss him."

"Yes," she said.

The nurse was still aiming mouthfuls, but now his mother turned her head completely away, and said her last, "Enough." So the nurse gave up and took away the tray, explaining that they had to force feed her.

His mother had been a fantastic cook. Her son certainly loved to eat. I had never made matzo ball soup, but enjoyed it when it was homemade. I thought gefilte fish was born in a jar. I wanted to have his baby. I doubted if he would ever get married. He was a great lover. I thought he would be a good father. I let him say good-bye to his mother alone. I waited down the hall where I couldn't hear their conversation, but could imagine her saying how I already *had* children. "Too old for you. You need a Jewish wife."

When he came out of his mother's room, he looked lovable and sad, sexy and vulnerable, beaten, yet also unbeatable. He looked better than any other man to me. I would do anything for him.

"Well," I said, walking towards him, taking his hand, "what did she say?"

"Nothing," he acted surprised.

"Didn't you ask about me?"

"No," he said.

After my father had met Mel, I wanted to know, "What did you think?" And my father had answered, "I liked him *very* much." I had expected no less, but now I wanted her approval.

"Why didn't you ask?" I wondered. "Don't you care what your own mother thinks?"

"Excuse Me," he said. But I was also offended, and he hated to see me upset.

"She thought you were pretty, and very nice," he went on. "Easy to get to know."

"Why say that? Why lie about it?"

"I doubt if she even knew you were here," he said.

The Answer

He couldn't decide if he should marry. He was already in his 40's, and he'd never been married. People said that he'd be a perfect partner except for this flaw. Being a bachelor had become a stigma. But for the last couple years, he'd had this idea that he wanted to get married. He even spoke of it the first time we met, though he wasn't referring specifically to us.

"What do you think you want?" he asked.

I said I'd be happy with a committed weekend relationship. "I'm not against marriage. I just don't believe in divorce."

But he thought he wanted a baby. Everybody else had a baby.

"But even if a child were conceived," I said, "we still wouldn't have to get married."

"Not with me kid," he said. He believed one got married first.

I began to wonder if he only wanted to get married because he thought he should. Or if he did get married, would he only be trying it on to see how it felt? Maybe he had doubts about me, if I were the right woman.

He admitted to friends that he wasn't sure. One friend admitted to me this admission. That friend said that I should sit him down and ask *him* to get married.

"No way, José," I answered.

Still, one night I confronted him. "Do you think we'll ever get married?"

"I don't know," he said.

"What don't you know. If I'm the right one?"

"I don't know," he said.

"Well then why don't you go ask God," I suggested.

He looked at me oddly. He was more likely to ask the cigarette he was smoking.

"Really," I smiled. "Just try it. Go in the other room and ask."

He got up slowly, then put out the cigarette and left the room.

I sat on the bed, thinking about what God would say to him. I imagined God would say, "Do you really think you'll find anyone better? Of course not. Go ahead." I had to believe in that answer.

Suddenly he returned. He was also smiling.

"What did He say?" I asked.

"He said no."

"That's funny." I must have looked disappointed. "That's not what He told me."

"What did He say to you?"

"I guess I didn't really ask," I admitted. "I was only trying to overhear your conversation."

"But," he paused, "I still want to marry you."

I looked at him blankly.

"What do you say?" he asked.

"How can I say yes, if God said no," I responded.

"He didn't really say No," he admitted. "I just made that up."

"So you didn't really ask?"

"I felt stupid," he admitted.

"That's all right. That's how you're supposed to feel. We *are* stupid."

"I'm not," he responded. And then he stood up. I thought he was going to leave. Maybe he had his answer, and it was over.

"Where are you going?" I asked.

"In the other room."

"What are you going to do?"

He walked to the door, and then looked at me, "I'm going to see if He changed His mind," he said.

The Trap

I told him I would never call him, though I'd always return a call of his. He thought that was silly, that I should call whenever I had something to say. Why put all the responsibility on him? But I knew better. I said, "If I got into the habit of calling you, you'd come to resent it. You'd think I was just checking up on you." And once he knew that I was capable of calling him, he would end up calling me less, waiting for my turn, until I'd break down and call him again, since I'd begun to do it anyway.

Today, Sunday morning, 10 a.m., I'm not calling to find out if he's at work, I'm calling to find out why he isn't. He's been working seven days a week for the past two months, trying to get this film cut. I ask the hotel operator for his room, and half expect him to answer, "hey," but a woman's voice has another impact.

"Is Mel there?" I ask.

She groans. I've awoken her. "I guess he left," she says. Brilliant.

"Is this Mona?" I ask, knowing that will awaken her.

I once teased him by saying he'd been moaning for "Mona" all night in his sleep, pure invention, but he retorted, "You mean Mona from the hospital?" For a second I didn't know if she were real or not.

"This is Jennifer," she answers. Sounds like one. "Do you want to leave a message?"

"Just tell him that Mona called," I say to further confuse things. "Tell him he has no need to call back. I'll come pick up my stuff. He can leave my coyote in the closet."

"Oh," she says. "I thought that belonged to his girlfriend."

Now it's my turn for confusion.

I have the key to his room in my wallet. It looks like a thin cardboard credit card, with a picture of a key and perforated holes—this is your modern key—not a real object, with character and weight, something that turns a real lock, no real true lasting love at the Sheraton. But I stick it down the slot one last time, watch the green light flash, then push down.

It had become more and more apparent that he didn't like the way I dressed. He made subtle comments at first, window shopping, "You'd look great in that," severe black outfits with radical skirts, clothes I'd have nowhere to wear. One time I got the look right, a blue-black oversized jacket with plenty of shoulders, tight black pants. He couldn't stop raving, "Just look at yourself. It's terrific. Now you look thirty-four, not like some kind of matron."

Suddenly I worried about age. Wrinkles became an obsession. I checked out everybody's face, the way lines had formed on older people, compared to mine, those just beginning etch marks, little crescents around the mouth. I was not a frivolous person, so why not accept some worry lines. I was a real person who did her own laundry. Mel worried about losing hair. He had plenty of it, and I couldn't care less, but he was a hawk for wrinkles. Vanity made him want me to look good.

I feel disgust for the burnt sienna which overwhelms the room — carpet, paper, drapes. The maid has been here already, tidy bed, clean ashtrays. In fact it doesn't even smell like smoke. Maybe he hasn't been sleeping here, didn't want to be around when I came to collect my stuff.

He certainly hadn't begged "Mona" for a second chance. I called him at work after my little conversation with Jessica.

"Hi hon, it's me," I say. For a second he's not sure who it is. I'm calling from Florida, supposedly in a sun-drenched mood. "How's your weekend going?" I ask.

"All right," he answers, distracted. I've interrupted him, I feel. Another reason why I don't like to call.

"You wouldn't believe my tennis," I say. "And I'm swimming fifty laps. I've never felt so fit."

"Are you getting tan?"

"Yes, but it makes me horny. Why do you have to work so hard."

"That's life," he says, resigned. "But this is a hectic time for me. I'm trying to finish the sound track with Neal."

"How was she," I ask. "I mean, your date."

"What is it with you," he sounds angry. He never answers questions like this one directly.

He'd said repeatedly how he hadn't slept with anyone else since the day he met me. I tried to overlook the messages left on his machine, "Oh Melly, I miss you *so much* . . . At the sound of *my* beep, leave a message on *my* machine . . . Take care of your beautiful self, Melvin . . ." or that simple, sweet, seductive, "hi . . ." as if the world should know who that is.

"You have no reason to be jealous," he states, "and frankly

I'm in no mood for it this morning."

"Mood!" I warn him, 'MOOD! I just wanted to let you know that I just spoke to Janicka." Silence on the other end. "You're so full of shit my head's running over!"

Silence on my end, breathing, deep battled breathing.

"You've got it all wrong. I can tell you're upset, but you're wrong."

"Oh yeah?" Dying for a believable excuse.

"I didn't sleep with her, I just let her use my room. I spent the night in Neal's other bed. She's up here for a dental conference."

"Why did she say you just left?"

"I went up to *change* this morning, ok? She's just an old college friend, ask Neal. The three of us had dinner together." He waited. "Kate?" I was waiting too. "If you can't believe me, what good is this."

"Listen, she told me everything. She was sleepy and had her defenses down. I threw her off balance by asking for Mona."

"Who?"

"We even laughed about your handsome *schlong*."

"You said *that*?"

"Do I need to reiterate what you already know? She even told me her bra size."

Once I had asked him, "Do you like big tits?" And he had said, "No, I hate them." But his male friends knew he liked "dairy," and I was skimpy on top, but Jennifer with her jambalayas, her boobs, her billowy cushions. I could picture him checking her out in the lobby, thinking— That woman's well put together— How he'd approach that part of her softly at first, but undressed he would almost ravish them— He'd suck them and squish them and push them together, adore them and look at them jiggle, and make them swing, and watch them hang— Milk them and pinch them and fuck them and take them, swallow them whole— Great Tits!

It is 10 a.m. Sunday morning, Eastern Standard Time for us both. I had bad dreams last night, a bout of insomnia, because he hasn't called in two days. I need to hear his voice. I break the rule I've made for myself and call him anyway. He answers, "hey." He is usually up for work by now.

"You told me to call when I had something to say, and you know how rare that is."

He makes an animal sound. I've awoken him. "I really tied one on last night," he admits. "I thought I could sleep it off." He's holding up a finger to his lips, indicating to the girl beside him that she should keep quiet. "Can I call you back," he says, "after I shower?"

"Well, I'm going to be out all day. We rented a boat. The boys want to fish."

But the girl is impatient, and I hear her whine, a rustle in the background, my excellent ears.

"What's that?" I ask.

"What's *what*," he answers.

"Someone's with you," I say.

"Will you knock it off, Kate. Nobody's with me."

"Liar," she whispers, loud enough for me to hear.

"I'll call you back," he says, squeezing her arm, she says, "Ow."

"No need to," I say, "not ever."

"Fine!" he yells, dropping the phone on the floor beside the bed, and I'm left there, listening, mutely listening as he proceeds to grapple with her. I hear their struggled tussling— He's tickling her and holding her down— her groans, her sighs, her stretching calls, being stroked and bent and taken. Then I get to hear her slobbering over him, her drooling, muttering, praising, her reaching lips all clasp and hunger, until his final, *"unnn."*

I often felt thirsty in this room of his. Maybe it was the altitude, or lack of real air. It felt like sleeping on an airplane. I bought a humidifier, which seemed to help, but now the room feels dry.

I tear the bedding from the huge, neat bed, trompling on it merrily. I get my hair curler set from the bottom drawer. He didn't like to see my hair done. He had gotten to that "admitting phase." He preferred my hair all messed up, wild looking, as if I'd spent the day in bed. Like when?

I stuff my clothes in the duffle, no time to fold, but the coat, my coyote, isn't hanging in the closet. Did he have the nerve to still wear it? That coat, made him look like a hunk with big shoulders, made him look like the filmmaker he was, with his torn t-shirt and three day beard. I loved the way he looked.

Calmly, deliberately, I wreck the room, sweep the side tables clean of spare change, empty cigarette boxes, cannister of pills, hotel information flying, then notice that my letters are gone. He had always left them out before, as proof of his fidelity, that no other girl could be brought to this room, with love notes prominently displayed.

I dump out the drawers, the neatly rolled t-shirts, socks, underwear. The hotel does his laundry. He never cooks food. Clean sheets and towels daily. It all makes me weary like excess of ease.

I place the key card on the naked bed. The bare mattress looks peculiar, virginal, like an unused diaphragm, rubbery and functional. The pillows are far and wide.

Shutting the door to the hotel room, I feel a momentary pang, a panic, that maybe I can get back in, put everything back together, remake the bed, forgive him, and I'd be there, napping when he returned, the humidifier breathing with moisture. I test the door. It's sealed. Now the humidifier's empty. I guess he doesn't fill it anymore.

I decide to call Neal from the downstairs lobby. I'll get him to make the exchange of coats outside their office building, blocks away. Neal will want to help prevent a scene.

"Don't say anything to Mel," I insist. "I just want what's mine, then I'm out of here."

Neal says, "O.K." I think he is secretly glad that it's come to this. Mel liked to call Neal, in joking, "My wife." Both of them found that amusing. They both found endless fault with most women, waitresses, editors, over-wrought girl friends. They had slept with too many to know what they wanted. Perhaps Mel needed some composite touch, taken from the very best qualities of all the women he'd ever been with. Well, I guess she's out there somewhere, with her teenage legs and high-fashioned mind, but she's getting older too.

When I reach the revolving door, Neal isn't waiting. The guard is sitting at the desk as usual. Silent, grey tomb of a place. Chilly. Then Mel walks out of the elevator with an unlit smoke in his mouth, wearing my coat, fucking *wearing* it! I back away as he revolves outward. I am too furious to speak. He lights the thing, and turns from me, as if I wanted to admire his profile. "You can have it, when I'm finished with this," he says, meaning the smoke, but I knock it out of his mouth.

"You *are* finished," I say. "Take it off."

He looks at me, imitating my very-mean-look, and slowly starts to unbutton it, lets it slide from his shoulders onto the ground. I drop his coat beside it, and then turning back suddenly whack him across the face. He trips backwards over the coat, knocks his hand hard against the concrete slab of wall, then cradles his arm as if injured.

"Hey," he says. "It's me."

"Hi," I answer, yawning.

"It's Sunday you know, and I missed you this morning."

"I miss you too."

"How are you?" he asks. "Getting sun burned?"

"I couldn't sleep last night."

"You should have called me," he insists.

"I didn't think you'd appreciate a press conference, not at 3 a.m."

"That's true," he chuckles. "How're the boys."

"They're fine, but I don't like travelling alone."

"You're not alone. Are you still coming home tomorrow? I have to go back to the hospital."

"Will you call me? I want to know what the doctor says."

"Sure, I'll call."

"You didn't, for two days."

"You know where I am."

I don't answer this.

"You sound upset."

"I'm just not smoking."

"Good, don't smoke."

"I love you," I say.

"Well I love you too," he answers, in a way that feels totally credible, not just miming me. "And I'm tired of working. Next trip we go together. I've got to get back in shape. Kate? Are you there?"

"Yes. I was just thinking."

"You think too much. Relax."

"I can't relax when you tell me to."

"You know I've been staying at this hotel for so long, we've got a cruise coming on our extended stay card or whatever this thing is."

"For two?" I ask.

"Just me and you," he rhymes, to put me in a better mood. "I'm going to take you around the world. How would you like that."

How to Get Your Own Way

I said, "You can either not do it, or you can sneak, or be open about it."

He said how he simply had no desire to fool around anymore, unconscious of girls' flirtations. But he also said how it wouldn't mean a thing, if he were off in Oklahoma, and a hot little number walked into the bar. Marriage in his mind was final. If I were unfaithful, that was it. But then again, he wouldn't mind my having a one night stand, if he were in Europe for a month.

"I've never had a one night stand," I said.

"You slept with me that first night."

"But I'd never done that before, not once in my life."

"So why did you then? Because I'm so cute?"

"Because I wanted you," was my unsculpted response. "Don't forget how you tricked me, saying how the bed was so cold, and couldn't we just spend the night together. I thought we'd just cuddle and kiss."

"Oh sure."

"I'm serious. But when you took your clothes off and I saw you, Oh Boy."

"And then you wrapped these long arms around me."

"And it wasn't just a one night stand," I reminded. Nine months had passed and we were apparently monogamous. Still I wanted some indication of the future — Marriage, kids. "You know we don't have to have a child," I said, knowing if I went in one direction, he'd go the other.

"Well what about what *I* want," he said.

"I'd like to have your baby."

"So you've got my whole future planned."

"I don't know what you're going to do," I responded. "Maybe you'll take that job in London."

This brought him closer. "But I'm starting to like all this country stuff."

Perhaps we don't want what we seem to say we want. When a person is presenting herself on a platter, desire is snuffed.

I liked to picture a girl being brought into a gathering of men. They were playing poker and smoking. Her boyfriend wanted to share her, and presented her to the leader, who told her to undress, pretty much ignoring her presence. She stripped down to her underwear, and he commented, "All of it." So she took off her bra and her panties. "Now go lie down over there," he kept dealing, "and spread your legs. We'll get to you when we're ready."

"I wouldn't mind you sleeping with Michael or Bernie. They're my two best friends, and we've slept with a lot of women in common."

"What do you think I am!" I protested, but then played along. "I suppose if you wanted me to."

"I'd kill them," he switched.

I didn't know exactly which was the real him, or maybe parts of both. I knew if I said, "You're free to sleep with anyone," he would be less inclined.

"I want you to be faithful," made him think about Chicago.

"I don't have many chances left," made him postpone the idea of a baby altogether.

The other day he took my hand in the kitchen. "I want to ask you something." He seemed so tender, so ready, as he led me to the bedroom, I thought he was going to pop the big question.

"Can I put it inside you," he asked, "just for a moment?" This was surely living in the present. But I liked him making this request, doing whatever he wanted when he wanted. I liked leaning forward on the bed, and letting him come in from behind.

"Are you comfortable," he kept asking, but my comfort level wasn't a necessary consideration. I liked him taking me like this without protection.

Later, when I reminded him, he denied the risk, leaving it in my lap.

"Why can't we just be together. I'm tired of living out here all alone."

"But the country's so spooky. There aren't any pool halls, and what am I going to do?"

"You don't love me," I said, turning away from him, wanting him to be more demonstrative.

"Maybe you don't like *me* as much as you think. Maybe demands push a person away."

"Do you want me to call you a taxi? I mean if you don't know what you want by now."

"I know what I want, but I'm the guy." So now he wouldn't even budge.

"I'm not keeping you here. I've got things to do."

"Like what?" he wanted to know.

"I'm going to go plant the garden."

"Can I help?" he asked.

"Only if you want to," I answered.

So I troughed the rows, and he sprinkled seed, and we covered them up and pressed down.

Who Knows

When I received Kate's note that said she was ten days late, I was also about seven days late, and thrilled, not so much for myself or for her, but for the amazing, unplanned synchronicity. I called her immediately to find out that Yes, she had taken the rabbit test. Positive.

"When the nurse announced the results, Mel yelled Great!"

"Great," I agreed.

"But no," she continued. "He thought I was positively *not* pregnant."

"Oh, I see. Not so great."

"Listen," Kate told me, "No one must know about this, not even Cynthia."

"How can we not tell Cynthia?"

"We just have to wait. I promised Mel I wouldn't tell anyone, because first of all, we're not quite sure, and I want him to feel like he can decide."

So Kate slipped off to have a secret lunch with her mother and spilled the baked beans. Even though Kate and Mel weren't married, this news made Kate's mother very happy.

But although Kate told her mother, she insisted that her mother tell no one, not even her father, and so meanwhile Kate's mother got desperate to relate the good news to someone, just to ease the burden of her happiness. What good is joy if you can't get rid of it a little!

I was very good and didn't let on, so that Kate could tell Cynthia herself, and then she told both of us that her mother now knew, but that Mel didn't know that her mother knew, and must not know, because the plan was, that she and Mel were going to tell Kate's parents together. Mel wanted to announce that he had decided to marry their daughter, and to give them a grandchild, all of which had to be received as Great News!

Although Cynthia now knows, we still can't tell Nancy, another best friend to all three of us. Even though I never did come right out and tell Nancy, when I said, "Poor Kate got sick last night at the concert," Nancy responded, "Well that's what happens when you're pregnant," and I went, "What?"

Cynthia said to me, "You're the one who is pregnant. *You're* the one who's supposed to be throwing up."

Nancy nodded slyly, "Listen girls. I've had an inkling of my own for a couple of weeks."

So we made Nancy promise not to tell anyone, especially not Kate. We didn't want our friend to mistrust us. So now Nancy knows, and Kate doesn't know, plus Kate's mother knows and Mel doesn't know, and neither does Kate's father.

But what if Nancy accidentally told Mel that Kate had told her mother, having to explain that it was just something a daughter couldn't keep back, but that he shouldn't let on that he knew that Kate's mother knew, so that Kate would finally be the only one who didn't know what.

Letter to Rain

in memory of my friend,
Bill Sydney

"Love, & work,
Were my great happinesses, that other people die the source
of my great, terrible, & inarticulate one grief."

Ted Berrigan
Last Poem

When a friend dies he passes from your outside life to your inside —
how contain it, this winter I come home to. How cry for him who's
expanded, and yet I will, I do. I call his number just to hear his
voice, normal on the tape for the last time. For a moment, it's him,
same as always, with his pleased chin leading him onward, his im-
petuous nature, leading. We gave each other the same advice —
"Don't push so hard," *don't push so hard,* "Lay back," *lay back,* "Act
normal." We encouraged each other to quit, stop smoking, but look
at you now, Bill, you've really quit. You chump, you jerk, you
deserter! I know you didn't choose to do this. You didn't give up,
just your heart did. Yeah, we were both aging drag queens, bitch-
ing in the back of the car, lost kids in our over-sized bodies, over-
achieving for love, perplexed when it didn't come to us. You helped
me get over my heartbreak. Why didn't you let me help you. If
I'd known the facts before you left with her, I would have stopped
you before your heart did. But I'll miss you, dammit, forgive me,
for feeling so lonely and terrible. I know you'd have had higher
instincts. I know where you are, you've compassion for me, for
all of us who really cared for you. Know that Jamie will also be
cared for, that our love for you will help shelter her. Her strength
is proof of your fathering, stern sometimes, but always there for
her, and if I teach her to drive a car this spring, I'll make sure she
doesn't imitate either of us. I want her to feel the freedom we felt,
leaning on each other in this wilderness. I know I can't lessen the
loss for her, only fifteen. I will tell her that it's best to grieve, to
feel it in the gut, unbearable. If we try not to think, it hits us
anyway, and knocks us down like blackened surf. We have no choice
but to go with it. We must simply let it take us, until the wave

229

itself is beached, and we are breathing still, with the knowledge in our sore wet bones, as it keeps on washing over us, until it becomes almost soothing, as I hope you were soothed on the shores getting tan, smoking those awful Salems. I'm still using the honey you gave me for Christmas, the same kind we put in our afternoon tea, those late winter days before the hearth fire, sun pouring in the long windows, making that snowscape seem cozy. What more could you ask from a friend, music and laughter, cups running over, making the phone ring, "It's me. You really won't believe the latest." I'll miss arguing about the bill, Bill. I didn't really mind paying more than my half, but you had the main course and I just had salad! I'll miss your contorted expressions, your frankness, meeting you in town for the movies. I insisted you *not* drive past her house. Still, I understood you were driven. We hated to see each other punished by love. Though I think someone good would have come to you, who would have seen the real man where he stood. I feel like I want to reach out for you, to meet you halfway — Instead I find this space, this gaping. A handful of flowers, yanked. You never would have been so careless. You sent me a bundle of yellow chrysanthemums, and they really cheered me up. We did that for each other, you know, made life a lot easier, not such a load, unloading to each other on the telephone, driving up to Pittsfield in your little red truck. I was always grossing you out, while you were so funny and proper. Brown swans glide upon the Zurich Zee, but now as I'm riding to your services, I see a huge flock of white swans spread out along the river, magical as an accompaniment. They seem elegant, aloof and reticent. Later, when the river freezes, a fisherman sits and looks down through augured ice. The other day I had this vision, how I could also sit there freezing, over the tiny hole I'd dug, or I could make the whole lake water, and be swimming on my back and truly breathing. With you gone, I have fallen out of balance. Is it possible for the dead to miss the living? I know I'll miss you in your kitchen in Alford, whipping something up, famous for your undercooked chicken. I'll miss your pink and blue glasses, your rides to the city with the tape deck turned up. You were the best big brother. I can't berate you anymore, or hear your good common sense. You were such a decent person, and I depended on you, did you know that? I keep seeing your face in real life. How you could dance on your tiptoes, when you were happy with a secret for a moment. I'd have to get it out of you, "What!" But will you be there for me, Bill, when my turn swings around? I know we'd have quite a reunion, something like lying out at Tanglewood, a musical heaven, having eaten so well, with permission to relax now on life. To think that you know, what not one of us can conjure, to fit the true picture you now fill, blooming like a giant chrysanthemum, expanding both inner and outer flying father and mother toward the heart as the petals open. When your human heart closed, those petals began their dilation. I'm sure of it, Bill, you took to it, breathless, plunged into that other element. So when I feel you come into this inner life of mine, it won't be alone with just emptiness, but alive with the light of you, open in the rain, with the relief of a good long rain. Like spring, which goes on living.

Printed October 1988 in Santa Barbara & Ann Arbor
for the Black Sparrow Press by Graham Mackintosh &
Edwards Brothers Inc. Design by Barbara Martin.
This edition is published in paper wrappers; there
are 300 cloth trade copies; 150 hardcover copies
have been numbered and signed by the author; & 26
copies handbound in boards by Earle Gray have been
lettered & signed by the author.